Green Profit®
on Retailing

Edited by

Rick Blanchette and Jayne VanderVelde

Ball Publishing
Batavia, Illinois
USA

Ball Publishing
335 North River Street
Batavia, IL 60510, USA
www.ballpublishing.com

Library of Congress Cataloging-in-Publication Data

Green profit on retailing / edited by Rick Blanchette and Jayne VanderVelde.
    p. cm.
  ISBN 1-883052-22-x (softcover : alk. paper)
   1. Ornamental plant industry. 2. Plants, Ornamental--Marketing. I. Blanchette, Rick,
1966- II. VanderVelde, Jayne, 1975-

SB443 .G77 2000
380.1'4159--dc21   99-057915

Printed in the United States of America
05 04 03 02 01 00 1 2 3 4 5 6

Contents

Contributing Authors

Teresa Aimone is a sales representative for the Henry F. Mitchell Company, King of Prussia, Pennsylvania.

George Ball Jr. is chairman of Ball Publishing, Batavia, Illinois, and W. Atlee Burpee Co., Warminster, Pennsylvania.

Chris Beytes is editor of *GrowerTalks* magazine and contributing editor for *Green Profit*, Batavia, Illinois.

Laurie Beytes is a horticulturist, Naperville, Illinois.

Sherri Bruhn is editor of *Seed Trade News* magazine and contributing editor for *Green Profit*, Batavia, Illinois.

H. Marc Cathey is president of the American Horticultural Society, Alexandria, Virginia.

Mike Cooling is director of Cooling's Nurseries, Knockholt, Kent, England.

Jennifer Derryberry is president of Grace Communications, Batavia, Illinois.

Tracy Dominick is a former production editor of *Green Profit*.

Mac Faulkner is national sales and marketing manager, Grower Division, The John Henry Company, and sales director of Idea Works, a department of creative horticulture marketing specialists at John Henry, Lansing, Michigan.

Janice Fleury, Buchbinder, Chicago, Illinois.

Douglas C. Green is the owner of Simple Gifts Farm, Athens, Ontario, Canada.

Dave Hamlen is the owner of Hamlen's Garden Center, Swanton, Vermont.

Debbie Hamrick is editor of *FloraCulture International*, and contributing editor for *Green Profit*, Batavia, Illinois.

Margaret K. Kelly is a freelance writer, Greenville, New York.

Peter Konjoian is president of Konjoian's Floriculture Education Services, Andover, Massachusetts.

Dr. Marvin N. Miller is market research manager for Ball Horticultural Company, West Chicago, Illinois.

Kim Moreland is a former editorial assistant at Ball Publishing.

Stan Pohmer is a consultant focusing on the floral and lawn-and-garden industries, Minnetonka, Minnesota.

Shirley Remes is a freelance writer, Elgin, Illinois.

J Saxtan is a former international editor of *Green Profit*.

Laurie Scullin is marketing manager, the Paul Ecke Ranch, Encinitas, California.

Joli A. Shaw is a freelance writer and former editor of *Green Profit*.

Ira Silvergleit is director of research and information for the Society of American Florists (SAF), Washington, D.C.

Gary Wittstock, Pond Suppliers of America Inc., Yorkville, Illinois.

Introduction

Darwinian Retailing

Consumers have more options available to them than ever before.

In the short history of humanity, we've gone from the barter system to purchasing items with valuable metals to a complex economic system where most of the money doesn't exist in hard currency. We started out raising or hunting what we needed to survive, trading our extras for needed or wanted items from a neighbor. Then as cities developed and currencies were created, we increasingly came to work for money to buy items we needed for survival and recreation, and we bought those items from farmers and craftsmen. The Industrial Revolution ushered in mass production, and we gradually bought fewer items from local artisans and more from stores where goods were shipped in from across the country—even from across the world. Today, thanks to the Information Revolution, we're able to purchase items we'd never dreamed of from places we've never heard of with money we never see. And we can get it delivered next day, for an additional delivery charge.

The point? Our world—and your business—is changing . . . quickly. The competition has not only increased, but evolved. No longer is the garden center or greenhouse competing only with the guy across town; in addition, he contends with the grocery store selling flats on its sidewalk, plus a big box or two, plus dozens of places across the country his customers can shop at with the click of a mouse. The local florist? He vies for customers with other local florists, supermarkets (some of which are offering floral delivery), chain florists such as Gerald Stevens, and Web sites featured on AOL and other Internet providers.

And your customers have evolved, too. They've become jaded to the same-old, same-old; they're immune to and suspicious of the hard sell. They often look at shopping as entertainment and more often are looking for a store that matches who they are and what they want to achieve. Many times image will win out over low prices—if your image is one your customers want to identify with.

We've collected the best articles from *Green Profit* magazine, and a few from our sister publication *GrowerTalks,* so you'll have in one place helpful suggestions and vital information about marketing, merchandising, customer service, the Internet, plant care, specialties like birding and water gardens, and tips on how to spot and take advantage of trends.

We hope you'll find *Green Profit on Retailing* a practical tool in your quest to stay at the top of the retail food chain.

Chapter 1
Customer Service

Are You Preparing for More Diverse Customers?

The American population is becoming more and more racially diverse, and savvy retailers are taking advantage of this expanding trend. According to Metropolitan Life data and Research Alert, by the middle of the next decade, the size of the U.S. minority population will equal the Caucasian population. During the first half of the 1990s, the minority population grew by 14 percent, compared to 3 percent for the Caucasian population. Hispanic and Asian populations grew the fastest, up 20 and 23 percent, respectively. The African-American population increased 8 percent in the same time period. It's projected that the Asian population will expand the most rapidly in coming years, while Hispanics will gain the most numbers.

As a flower and plant retailer, how can you effectively meet the needs of these expanding customer bases? First, know the traditional holidays: Japanese and Chinese New Years' celebrations, African-American Kwanza (celebrated December 26–31), Hispanic Semana Santa (Easter) and Dia de los Muertos (Day of the Dead, October 30).

Keep each culture's important holidays and colors in mind. Red callas in a red or black vase would be perfect for Kwanza.

Second, know the important colors. For the Chinese, red is a color of celebration. The Japanese consider red and white important. African-Americans use red, green, and black for Kwanza. Hispanics use a wide range of colors to celebrate, from traditional white for Easter to red for Mother's Day. Mexican markets are often decorated with white, red, and yellow.

In plants and flowers, Asians use large mum flowers for many traditional holidays and flower-giving events. Pine boughs, bamboo, and flowering quince are also important, especially at New Year's celebrations. The thirty-one-year-old holiday Kwanza has no traditional flowers, but native African flowers such as gerberas, freesias, proteas, and calla lilies could be marketed for this event. Hispanics celebrate Easter with traditional white flowers such as calla lilies, while for Dia de los Muertos, they create church ornaments from long-stemmed orange marigolds. It's also important to know a bit about ethnic cuisine so you can carry the appropriate selection of herbs, vegetables, and fruit trees.

While other industries, such as greeting cards and gift wrap, have begun to find ways to offer the traditional colors and patterns these ethnic groups want, floriculture is just beginning to learn to market to them. But a little bit of research can go a long way toward better serving *all* of your customers.

Consumer Buzz, September/October 1997.

Eight Things Consumers Don't Know about Flowers and Plants

H. Marc Cathey

Talk radio is a trip into a world where the consumers have already become horticulturally correct. They want healthy, clean plants to grow. This is a critical fact, even when the green industries continue to market their products without trademarked names, without identified patented germplasm from genetic engineering, without correct Latin names and universal coding, and without even the labeling of who produced/grew the plants. I have been hosting a weekly two-hour talk show on gardening every Saturday morning for about twelve years. We capture roughly one million listeners from Maryland, Pennsylvania, Ohio, West Virginia, Virginia, the District of Columbia, Delaware, and North Carolina from a forty-three-station network. I chart twenty-five calls per week; thus I have answered more than 15,600 questions during my radio career. What are the top questions/problems I solve again and again?

Right Plant/Right Place

Consumers continue to buy plants that do not succeed in their zone. The USDA Hardiness Plant Zone classifications are a mathematical treatment of the average minimum winter temperature at almost 10,000 weather stations, from Zone 1 (-50°F) in ten-degree increments to Zone 11 (40°F). This simplified coding appears in catalogs and garden books, but seldom on plant labels—and that can lead to mistakes in consumer buying.

Answer: Code plants with a geographical designation and teach the best locations and care required for each plant species.

Root Rots

Once gardeners find a plant, a color, and a look that gives pleasure, they tend to plant the site with exactly the same selections year after year. Particularly when the plants are petunias and impatiens, they do not thrive after a few years. Gardeners, in desperation, usually put on more water-soluble fertilizer, water more frequently, and heavily mulch the site; they, in fact, create a perfect site for root rots.

Answer: Rotate plantings, add gypsum (five pounds per one hundred square feet), apply a three-inch layer of organic matter yearly, and reduce fertilizer and watering to help make the area productive again.

Colonies of Insects and Diseases

Overwintered garden plants are often the yearly source of insects (thrips, red spiders, whiteflies, aphids, and scales) and diseases (rots of all kinds). The dim and stressful indoor environment may not favor their development, but the residue and potential for rapid expansion remains.

Answer: Start each year with new color plants. Check for flying dandruff, and use only spot-free plants. A healthy year begins with healthy plants.

Water

Although tap water is fine for most plants, it may contain low levels of chlorine, salts, particles, and calcium carbonates that are harmful to plants. Water also contains oxygen, carbon dioxide, and many trace amounts of other gases. Municipal water usually works fine, even with all of these foreign substances in it. Plants that are extremely sensitive to tap water are lilies, many foliage plants, African violets, most ferns, and mosses and primitive families of plants.

Answer: Use rain water or distilled water on sensitive plants to encourage development of blemish-free plants.

Cut Flowers

Many traditional bedding plants such as petunias, zinnias, marigolds, snapdragons, and verbenas have also been used as a source of cut flowers for the home. Now the consumer is becoming progressively surprised that the already-in-flower bedding plants never outgrow their compact growth. These almost stunted plants may be the result of breeding, but more often are the result of overtreatment with growth regulators.

Answer: Grow cut flowers from seed in your own garden. The mix seed types, which are not hybrids, tend to be tall.

Special Cultivars

Every year, garden magazines feature enticing new hybrid flowers and foliage plants. When consumers go to their garden center to purchase plants, more times than not they encounter plants labeled only as to color, followed by a twenty-five-word general care tag. New cultivars are hard to find unless consumers shop with a local independent grower/seller at higher prices than at no-brand mass outlets.

Answer: Order special cultivars from seed catalogs, and grow your own under fluorescent lamps.

Genetic Engineering

Most consumers do not understand the genetic changes that have been realized for tomatoes or wheat, or even cows for that matter. They do know, however, that they want to grow or consume plants that are safe to handle or eat and that no new toxic agents will escape into our environment.

Answer: Genetic engineering speeds up the progress of finding stress-free and productive plants. I believe that nature has abiding laws that ensure the continued survival of plants.

Native Plants

This is the most explosive issue of all. The Clinton administration recommends using native plants in landscaping government facilities. Until we have an agreement on a set of definitions and sources of exceptional native plants, the debate will continue to boil. Meanwhile, our industry must be careful not to introduce invasive or weedy plants while maintaining pest-free planting stock.

Answer: The green industries have a much higher priority than consumers do to provide the best plants. Otherwise, no one will buy their products.

Your Best Answer

Volunteer to sponsor and go on your local garden talk radio show. Get ready to hear how it truly is with the gardening consumer, and be prepared to begin your real education as a gardener.

GrowerTalks, *July 1995.*

Guarantees, Knowledgeable Staff Attract Customers

Plant-buying consumers want guarantees on plants, and they most prefer shopping at garden centers that offer good cultural advice, according to a survey by the Canadian Sphagnum Peat Moss Association. In the survey of one thousand households, nearly 90 percent of respondents said they'd shop more often at a store that offered guarantees on perennials, trees, and shrubs, even if another store was more convenient.

Fear of failure discourages many potential plant purchases. The survey showed that 50 percent of plant purchasers often hesitate to buy new plants, especially expensive varieties, for fear the plants will die. However, the chance to learn about the plants they're buying attracts customers to some garden centers. More than 70 percent of survey respondents said they shop at garden centers where the sales staff offers cultural advice.

If your garden center offers a guarantee, make sure customers are aware of it. And make sure your staff members know what they're selling. Consider hiring master gardeners, garden club members, college horticulture students, or other plant-savvy employees.

Consumer Buzz, July/August 1997.

Retail Service from the Customer's Perspective

Joli A. Shaw

If Wal-Mart carries the plants you sell, Bookland carries the books you sell, and Lowe's sells the same shovel you sell, why should customers spend their money at your retail establishment? What's your competitive edge?

Perhaps it's service quality, which depends on balancing expectations and perceptions. At the Ohio Florists' Association's Short Course in July, Bridget K. Behe, Auburn University, Auburn, Alabama, revealed what recent surveys have discovered about consumer perceptions and expectations of retail service.

SERVQUAL, a survey instrument developed by Zeithaml, Parasuraman, and Berry, defines five dimensions of service quality: tangibles, reliability, responsiveness, assurance, and empathy. In recent surveys, Wayne Becker used an adapted SERVQUAL to assess service quality at traditional florists and supermarket floral departments in Texas, and Jay Hudson used SERVQUAL to assess service quality at traditional garden centers and mass-market garden outlets. Both asked customers to allocate one hundred points to each of the five service dimensions to identify how important each was. Then customers rated their expectations and perceptions of their own retail outlet.

What Customers Want

Garden center customers valued assurance (knowledgeable employees who convey trust) and responsiveness (prompt help) as most important, yet both retailers had an assurance service quality gap, Bridget says. The traditional retailer has an edge and can further develop it. Mass marketers can close the gap.

In contrast, florist customers valued reliability (dependable, accurate service) and responsiveness (prompt help) over assurance, empathy, and the tangible aspects of service quality. The traditional florist had no service quality gap, but the supermarket retailer did. It wouldn't take much effort to close the gap, she says.

Relative importance of five service quality dimensions as rated by traditional and nontraditional garden center and florist customers

Dimension	Garden center customers		Florist customers	
	Traditional Points (Rank)[1]	Nontraditional Points (Rank)[2]	Traditional Points (Rank)[1]	Nontraditional Points (Rank)[2]
Assurance	26 (1)	25 (1)	17 (3)	16 (5)
Responsiveness	24 (2)	24 (2)	22 (2)	22 (2)
Empathy	21 (3)	19 (3)	15 (4)	20 (3)
Reliability	17 (4)	17 (4)	33 (1)	24 (1)
Tangibles	12 (5)	15 (5)	13 (5)	16 (5)

[1] Average points for all participants
[2] Based on the Wilcoxon rank-sum test

GrowerTalks, *In Brief, September 1996.*

Edutainment

Stan Pohmer

As retailers increasingly look for opportunities to differentiate themselves, they usually focus their attention on prices, assortments, and sometimes presentation. Dealing with product that's perishable, we need to do whatever we can to educate consumers on how to take care of our products once they get them home. If we can accomplish this, they'll have a more enjoyable experience with what they've purchased and will be more prone to come back and buy our product again. It's to our selfish advantage to make consumers as smart as we can so they have the knowledge necessary to care for and maintain the plants. But this knowledge is sometimes difficult to deliver, especially in the mass markets.

Also, consumers today have been brought up in the MTV era, where they're conditioned to having information delivered in sound and visual bites that are both pleasurable and enjoyable. Webster defines *entertainment* as "that which engages the attention agreeably and amuses, the hospitable provision for the wants and needs of a guest." Taken in a broad sense, today's consumers want to be entertained when they shop; they demand that shopping be a "fun" experience.

Combining both elements results in what's labeled as "edutainment" (a form of entertainment that's designed to be educational) or "shoppertainment" (a combination of leisure and shopping, focusing on an experience as value). If we take advantage of consumers' needs for knowledge in a fun shopping environment, supported by great assortments, we'd be amazed at how much floral and garden product we can sell.

Real World Examples

All you have to do is look around, and you'll see examples of retailers delivering edutainment. For instance, Lowe's and Target participate in local market home and patio shows, providing products (and staff) to design interior and exterior vignettes in model homes that highlight the current trends in floral and lawn and garden, as well as keying in on their current assortments. Think about it: Consumers pay to gain entrance to these shows for the opportunity to be educated and trained in pleasant surroundings!

I've seen many great displays in supermarkets that were dynamic in delivering a message while really catching my eye. Some sidewalk and parking lot floriculture events that I've seen had supplier experts on hand to provide quality information in a carnival-like atmosphere. It was enjoyable just watching people having fun spending their money!

What's the secret to making this happen? First, successful retailers have a real understanding of who their customer is. Next, they know their mission and the message they want to deliver. Last, they create and develop a means of delivery that works within their operating environments, one that makes the shopping experience fun.

I'm not suggesting that you turn your floral department or garden center into a Disneyland or a Coney Island (though it would be interesting to see consumers' reactions), but I am challenging you to look for every chance to deliver education and training to our consumers. And I'm also challenging you to make the shopping experience *fun* for the customer.

Pohmer's Perspective, January/February 1998.

Consumers Want Value . . .

Joli A. Shaw

"Value conscious." The phrase is becoming another buzz phrase in the industry, used by trend watchers everywhere to show that they're in touch with consumers and have their fingers on the pulse of the industry.

Hand in hand with this thirst for value is a hunger for the innovative, the fun. Big-box retailers have fueled consumers' expectations for myriad choices; independents have stoked their desire for the unusual and the entertaining. To consumers, these characteristics—many choices that are entertaining—comprise value.

But are any retailers really taking advantage of this value-conscious phenomenon? For the most part, no, says Leonard Berry, professor of marketing and director of the Center for Retail Studies in the College of Business Administration at Texas A&M University. "Some have, but there are a great many retailers who are very loathe to respond," he says in *Inside Retailing.* "Tired stores, uninteresting stores, stores with uninspired merchandise selections—a little bit of this and a little bit of that—stores with order takers, not salespeople."

Unfortunately, this statement can be applied to many of the garden centers and floral departments consumers see when shopping today. Consumers want more, and they want better. They want to see sixty types of flowers and plants, and they want each of them to be the best quality possible. And when these plants don't last, consumers notice. To today's plant shopper, vase life is value.

Consumers want value, and thus quality, but they want it conveniently. In other words, they want that spectacular *Dieffenbachia,* but they don't want to have to fuss over it every day—they've got enough to worry about with picking the kids up from soccer and ballet. Thus, many growers and manufacturers are taking steps not only to make their product easier for the consumer to care for, but also to give it a higher perceived value. Hermann Engelmann Greenhouses, for example, has introduced its Water Magic system for the foliage plants for which it's famous. A funnel inserted into the plant medium takes the guesswork out of watering plants by gradually, automatically distributing water to plants as they need it.

Consumers want value, and they're willing to pay for it. As Leonard says, "To the consumer, value is benefits received for burdens endured: what I get for what I have to endure to get it." Here we're talking not only about the monetary expense for the product, but also about the perceived value in that price. Thus, the potential sales in a long-stemmed red rose bouquet labeled "Red-hot romance, $49.99" instead of "Roses, $49.99."

Attracting consumers on price alone is fine for a while, but the cheapest poinsettia is not necessarily what consumers look for—today's plant consumers are value conscious. Consumers are beginning to make the connection between three-dollar plants that last three to five days less than the eight-dollar plants. In many cases, they want the price, but they want the value more. Make no mistake: Low price does not equal value.

In My Opinion, January/February 1998.

What Women Shoppers Want—and Don't Want

Women shoppers look not only for specific products when they shop, but also for specific environments and experiences, according to consultant Linda VanWilgen at a presentation at the Southeast Greenhouse Conference. With a majority of garden center customers being women, are you meeting their needs and expectations? Or are you turning them off?

What women shoppers want:

- Intimacy, escape, and adventure
- The means to a simpler life
- New products
- Pleasant atmospheres
- Pampering
- Quick shopping for "have to buy" items

What women shoppers don't want:

- High prices and inconsistencies
- Lack of good selection
- Advertised products that aren't available
- No sales staff, especially no knowledgeable staff
- Unreasonable return policies
- Few, or slow, home deliveries
- Having to wait in line
- Stores that aren't child friendly
- Poor or outdated signage
- No place to sit or socialize
- No clean restrooms
- Not enough product information
- Dark, dirty stores

Consumer Buzz, November/December 1998.

It's a Guy Thing Too

George Ball Jr.

Let's face it, guys, what are our leisure-time options—that is, those that don't involve a sofa and a bag of potato chips? There's hunting, fishing, touch football, cards, bowling—and it's downhill from there. Many of these activities are expensive, dangerous, tedious, or all of the above. However, there's one inexpensive, safe, deeply satisfying hobby that is a little-known hit with a large number of men: gardening, especially vegetable gardening. I know— I've got the numbers. More than 50 percent of Burpee's mail-order customers are men, and vegetables account for more than half of their purchases. When I first discovered this and got over the initial shock, I was surprised that men buy this many plants. As a retailer, you have an untapped market that you can cash in on with a bit of targeted effort.

Men garden not only in high numbers, but also with great regularity, especially in lawn care and fertilizer and in both flowers and vegetables. This means men are a safe bet as customers once you get them to make an initial purchase. While retailers devote vast amounts of floor space to decorative garden gifts and spring-flowering plants oriented toward women, they pay little attention to vegetable plants and seeds, which will draw the men. Therefore, frequently the "green" shopper turns out to be a woman. After lugging bags of grass seed to the car, the men go off to look at hardware. This is a big mistake, especially for the small retailer.

Why ignore the other half of the market? Consider positioning your vegetable plants near the lawn seed and fertilizer displays to keep the men in the live goods section. Display signage there announcing your latest shipments of vegetable plants.

Vegetable plants displayed near this area would have increased men's purchases at this retailer.

Flowers tend to advertise themselves, so experiment in your garden section by adding more vegetable signs in your plant displays. Try promotions and easy in-store contests, like a "largest pumpkin" competition or a contest for photos of your kids or grandkids in the garden. (Men are always taking photos.) Try giveaways with every tray of vegetable plants—a pack of tags or a marker, for example. Tell your vendors about your interest in running a special promotion, and watch them compete to get to the front of the line to see you.

Another idea: Take tips from other retailers. My favorite example is Orvis, the fly-fishing giant. Truthfully, who has ever tied his own fishing flies? After shopping at Orvis, you'd think it was common. This is a pretty neat trick, as I work at a company with several hundred men and couldn't find a single fly fisherman. Orvis accomplishes this magical effect by employing a full-time fly-tying expert who sits in the middle of the product display area, making fishing flies while talking with customers. Considering their prices, it isn't surprising they can afford it in their budget. However, why can't plant retailers find more gardeners among their seasonal employees to help to promote the product line? The Home Depot and Hechinger's have promoted specialized customer service for years. Why can't more retailers catch up and cater to men who buy vegetable plants in far greater numbers than they buy specialty fishing flies?

Just remember that the men in your market could buy as many seeds and flowers as the women—and probably more vegetables. Be there with your promotions when they walk through your door.

George, March/April 1998.

Mature Customers Want What *All* Customers Want

With baby boomers getting on in years, it's important that your retail environment takes into account the needs of customers who may not be as willing or able to leap over puddles and step past garden hoses. Retail consultant Linda VanWilgen offered these tips to retailers at the Southeast Greenhouse Conference. We think they're such common-sense ideas that they apply to all retail environments and all customers. Look at your facility with a critical eye, then make the needed changes:

- No wet or slippery floors: Who needs a lawsuit?
- No steep steps: Ditto.
- Easy-to-maneuver carts: Wobbly wheels are for sitcoms.
- Good lighting: You can't buy what you can't see.
- Easy-to-reach product: No one likes a strained back.
- Seating/socializing area: Park benches are wonderful!
- Carryout service: Convenience is key.
- Less background noise: It's annoying to everybody.
- Paved parking: Mud holes are the pits.
- Covered shopping area: Rain-or-shine shopping!

Consumer Buzz, January/February 1999.

Who Buys Bedding Plants, Where, and Why?

Ira Silvergleit

The typical American bedding plant purchaser is a female homeowner who is fifty-five years old or older and has an annual household income of $50,000 to $60,000. Geographically, consumers in several clusters of states purchase more bedding plants: Texas, Oklahoma, Arkansas, and Louisiana;

Washington, Oregon, and California; and Wisconsin, Illinois, Indiana, Ohio, and Michigan.

Based on four years of data gathered from the American Floral Endowment's Consumer Tracking Study, consumers who purchase at garden centers (33 percent) say they do so most often because of product quality and selection, followed by price and convenience. Garden centers have lost 3 percent of market share over the last four years. They tend to attract middle-aged, affluent customers and are losing strength with younger, less affluent buyers.

Home improvement stores draw 15 percent of buyers because of convenience, shoppers say. Stores attract consumers who are between forty and fifty-four and 65 and older, as well as more affluent bedding plant buyers. Home improvement and hardware stores gained 3 percent market share since 1993, probably for the most part due to an increasing number of outlets.

Discount stores are where 18 percent of buyers purchase bedding plants, mainly because of price, they say. Market share for discount stores has been stable.

Supermarkets sell bedding plants to 8 percent of buyers. Convenience is the No. 1 draw, followed by price. They attract younger purchasers who buy primarily on impulse. Supermarkets have lost 2 percent market share of bedding plant sales since 1993.

Consumer Buzz, July/August, 1997.

Chapter 2
Marketing 101

Part 1:
Planning for Success

Mac Faulkner

Every day, more and more businesses—at every level in our industry—are getting involved in branding and marketing. What's driving this trend? Who's behind it? And, even more important, why are they doing it?

Two trends answer all three of those questions: consumer demand and increasing competition. Today's consumers are demanding more information and added value before they buy. So competition is increasing as horticulture businesses strive to differentiate themselves and satisfy consumers' demands.

What Motivates Your Customers?

Today's consumers aren't like their parents. They're more educated. They have less time. They're value-driven, and they're shoppers. Thanks to marketing successes like Nike, Starbucks, McDonald's, and thousands of others, they've been conditioned to respond to marketing stimuli. They've learned to develop loyalties and to shop by brand name, price, style, size, and shape; and they've learned an important concept called "value-added benefits." Those are the little extra things you do to not only meet but also exceed your customers' expectations.

Today's consumers choose wisely about where and how they're going to spend their hard-earned dollars, based on what they get in return. Often, that return is based on intangible "image" benefits—and the seeds of that image have been planted by marketing.

Today's consumers are part of the information generation. They're bombarded by publications, including many devoted to landscaping and gardening topics. They've got the Internet, home satellite dishes, and cable TV with hundreds of channels, one of which is dedicated to home and gardening twenty-four hours a day.

The current national boom in gardening as a favored leisure-time activity is creating big profit opportunities. But to capitalize on this trend you need to: Reach consumers in ways

that they're conditioned to respond to, give them the information they want and must have before they buy, and make them more successful in their landscaping and gardening projects.

The need for marketing and branding is heightened by consumers' ever-increasing demand for information, especially when it comes to helping them create the gardens of their dreams. They want to know which species will attract hummingbirds and butterflies. How high and wide the plants will get. When they'll bloom and for how long. Which new plants will complement what they're already growing. They want to know about textures, not just colors. They want design ideas and selection recommendations from companies and brands that they can trust.

When they have all of this information, they're ready to buy. Are you ready to help them buy from you?

Step One: The Business Plan

Do you want to attract customers to your products, excite them, sell to them, and then sell more to them? The first and most important step is to create a business plan for your success.

It's a cliché, but it's true: No one ever plans to fail; they simply fail to plan. In today's competitive marketplace, everyone needs a sound business plan. A plan provides both short-term seasonal gains and long-term benefits.

Without a plan, your efforts become reactive rather than proactive, and in today's competitive environment, you can't afford that. You need to control how consumers perceive you. By executing a sound business plan, you'll be positioned as a leader, not a follower.

What's in the plan?

A solid and effective business plan needs the following components:

- Market analysis (information gathering/defining your customers' needs)
- Business goals and objectives
- Promotional strategy
- Timeline
- Budget
- Goals analysis and measurement tools

We'll discuss the market analysis and your business goals in this article.

Market analysis

We all need to be aware of what influences are driving the purchasing decisions of today's consumers. What are the current trends? What do they indicate for our business now and in the future?

The answers are as close as your employees, your computer, your TV screen, and your bookstore. What are your cashiers and delivery people hearing customers ask for? Ask them. What are consumers reading about in *Better Homes & Gardens*? What are they seeing on HGTV? What are Martha Stewart and other lifestyle gurus promoting?

Read and watch what your customers are reading and watching. Then provide product that corresponds with the current trends in lifestyles, colors, sizes, shapes and the special value-added benefits they're looking for.

Simply looking at last year's sales won't do it, as trends are always changing. Just because something sold well this year doesn't mean it will sell well next year. We need to do a much better job of matching our product offerings with today's trends and what consumers want, rather than simply trying to unload product. Market analysis will help us do it.

Beyond the consumer media, there are many other resources that can help you gain valuable industry information and identify market trends. These include the Color Marketing Group, the Internet, USDA publications, trade publications, industry newsletters, and trade association bulletins.

Outside of industry information, there's a wealth of business and marketing publications available. Marketing is a science with many disciplines, outlined in many books available at your local bookstore. (A good cross-section of the disciplines can be found in Part 3, beginning on p. 26.)

Next, take a look at what you're growing, along with new crops and varieties that might satisfy today's consumer demand for all the new and different styles of gardening and landscaping. Water gardens, butterfly gardens, perennial specialties, meadowlands, "moon gardens," and many other collections are making the news today.

As noted industry authority Ian Baldwin said recently in a speech: "We're no longer in the 'nursery' or 'annuals' or 'perennial' industries—we're all in the 'garden decoration industry.'"

You could add that what we're selling is "home lifestyle satisfaction." Today's consumers are seeking a return to simple pleasures. With our beautiful products, we can satisfy the basic human needs of consumers to nurture and beautify their surroundings and help them to take pride in their accomplishments.

As another part of your market research, it's important to know what your competition is up to. Visit them and see what they're doing. Stay aware of what they're growing, how they're selling it, and who's buying it and why. Then decide who and what you want your business to be—and the best way to go about it.

Business goals and objectives

Ask yourself this question: "Who and what do I want my business to be to that ultimate buyer, the end consumer?" Do you want to be a generic, no-name plant provider? Do you want to be known as a trendsetter? Do you want to be the expert in new perennial varieties? The complete resource for water gardens? Your answers to these questions will help to establish your business image and identity.

Operationally, you need to cover all the bases in terms of service, delivery, pricing, etc. But in promotional marketing, you need to pick one thing you want to be known for so you can differentiate yourself in the marketplace and in consumers' minds. You can't be all things to all people. It's too expensive, for one thing. Instead, you should select one image focus, promote it, follow through on it, and support it with good business practices.

Once selected, your business identity needs to be promoted everywhere, every day—on letterhead, invoices, tags, banners, signs, vehicles, etc. In the next article we'll review the complete range of promotional tactics available. But for now, suffice it to say that establishing your point of distinction and promoting your business identity is a critical first step in achieving your business goals.

Of course, you also need to set realistic business objectives for your sales results (both short- and long-term), including your service and facility operations, inventory, and distribution channels, as well as your marketing promotions. Each business component relates to the other, and some may indicate the need for staffing at different levels. How well you integrate everything will affect the ultimate success with your business plan and its results in the marketplace.

Three other objectives should be specifically identified in your business plan, including whom you want to reach (your target markets), your timeline, and budget parameters. (Timelines and budgets are discussed starting on p. 25.)

Who's your target?

Consumer markets today are becoming more segmented; the masses are breaking down into niche markets. You need to establish promotional strategies that position you for success in your market niche and present product in the best possible way to reach your target consumers.

Targeted, niche marketing is one way that smaller outlets can compete with "the big guys." Without going through layers of organizational approvals, you can change your marketing approach as necessary. You can decide to become the price or service leader, the customer education resource, or the highest quality producer—proving it with a satisfaction guarantee.

In a nutshell, you need to identify and target your customer market, recognize why and how they buy, then promote your products in ways they'll respond to.

The best way to build gardeners' loyalty is to create success for them. Success with their shopping experience in terms of time, information, product availability, and convenience. A sense of fun and discovery in a colorful and stimulating environment. A feeling of pride in making a variety of appropriate selections and, ultimately, success with their plantings.

We can't always be on the retail floor physically. And we can't be at consumers' homes when they're using our products. But with a well-developed and focused business plan—supported by appropriate marketing strategies—we can most assuredly be with consumers when and where they're ready to buy. And isn't that right where we want to be?

Five Steps to Success

Mac Faulkner

1. Prepare and plan. Write down your goals, your sales objectives, and strategies in a business plan. Read it frequently. This will help you visualize and stay focused on your marketing success.
2. Turn on the creative power. Today's consumers expect it—and they respond to it. Look to resources like seed companies for promotional help or tag companies as a creative source. If you need to hire a free-lance marketing consultant or an outside advertising agency to power up your promotions, do it. Remember, it's a business investment, not an expense.
3. Turn on the people power. Hire the best people you can; continually train and upgrade them. Keep your staff informed about all business and marketing plans, from the top down. Give them a feeling of ownership in the process and in financial rewards for contributing to the growth of your business.
4. Push, protect, and pay. Once you've committed to a plan, stick with it. Be willing to invest both your time and financial resources. Push the system. Work it well. And give it time to evolve. If you initially experience a loss, deduct it as a business expense and chalk it up to the learning curve. Remember, skimpers don't win.
5. Enjoy. Make it fun to compete. And celebrate your successes!

GrowerTalks, *January 1999.*

Part 2:
Where to Advertise, How Much to Spend

Mac Faulkner

A few years ago, Riverbend Nursery in Riner, Virginia, a wholesale perennial, groundcover and ornamental grass producer, felt the effects of increased competition in the seven Mid-Atlantic states in which they sell. They decided to do something about it.

Owner Jim Snyder and his staff agreed that they should aggressively attract the attention of end consumers and pull in more sales by building a larger, more loyal customer base.

"We felt that if we could provide more complete and helpful product information, it would make Riverbend products the products of choice by consumers," Jim says. To that end, Jim and his staff came up with the B.I.G. Tag, which stands for Big Informative Guide.

"By going to a larger tag, we felt we could combine the information we were providing on our variety-specific bench cards with the standard information we were already printing on our tags," Jim explains. "This way, we could give consumers the point-of-purchase information they always want and need to know. Essentially, we would be sending a salesman and expert gardener with every pot."

Riverbend worked with John Henry's Idea Works department to develop the B.I.G. Tag and a complete marketing effort to support it. To introduce the B.I.G. Tag, Riverbend produced a one-page flyer to use as a handout at trade shows. They also mailed a flyer along with each of their catalogs and created a custom envelope that highlighted the B.I.G. Tag information inside. A new trade show booth was created to echo the "big" theme by featuring giant pots with giant tags. Riverbend has also begun to place advertising for their B.I.G. Tags in industry trade publications.

"It's a pretty major campaign for us," Jim admits. "But our season has been great, and it's still going strong. And, best of all, the consumer response has been terrific."

Let's Promote!

Riverbend used a range of promotional tactics to send the word out about their new product. Here's a review of various ways you can get your message across, win more customers, and earn more sales.

Personal selling

Of course, nothing beats the one-on-one relationships that are built with old-fashioned personal sales and service. But staffing is often lean and, especially during your busy seasons, it can be a challenge to get quality time with every customer. You need to find other avenues that enable you to build one-on-one relationships with today's gardening consumers.

Advertising

Advertising is a form of communication that delivers your sales message to potential customers when they aren't in your place of business. It's an investment, not an expense. When effective, it persuades buyers to seek out your brand and motivates them to purchase your products.

There are three types of traditional advertising: print, broadcast and outdoor. (The growing popularity of electronic advertising on the Internet will be discussed in Part 3 beginning on p. 26.)

Print advertising includes newspapers, magazines, yellow pages, and other business or consumer publications such as directories and school yearbooks.

Newspapers

Newspapers generally reach a wide audience at a reasonable price. People use their newspapers as an information resource. Your printed advertisement can be kept and referred to when needed. Newspapers also offer the greatest immediacy; a timely way to promote special sales and to push products and services in response to competition.

- Newspaper advertising can often be targeted geographically through regional editions; you only pay to reach the customers you want to reach.
- Most offer reduced rates if you run the same ad, with no copy changes, within a seven-day period.
- Sunday circulation is usually higher than daily, and readership is greater. Most papers offer a daily and Sunday advertising combination rate so you can get a better overall value.

Magazines

Trade and local magazines and business directories are great advertising vehicles, but only when they reach your target audience. Carefully analyze the editorial content of magazines you think you might want to advertise in. Ask for the magazine's media kit. It will tell you how many and what types of people are reading the magazine, how much it costs to advertise, and much more.

- Magazine advertising is generally more expensive than newspapers.
- You'll get a better rate if you sign a contract up front based on multiple ad insertions.
- Be sure to request good placement of your ad in each issue. Far-front, upper right-hand pages get the most attention from readers.
- Most magazines offer a reader service card as a way to track response to your advertising. Be sure to ask about it.

Yellow pages

Yellow-page advertising is different from any other type of advertising because of the way it's used. Consumers consult their yellow pages when they have a pretty good idea of what they want, but are not sure where to get it. Here are some guidelines to follow when planning effective yellow-pages ad design and placement:

- Your business name and telephone number must be prominently displayed.
- Boldly display any slogan or emblem that identifies and distinguishes your business.
- Show your hours of operation.
- Include a map or detailed directions to your location(s).
- If it's a selling point, include your years in business. Reliability is important.
- List some benefits of your products. Remember, we're in the "home lifestyle satisfaction" business!
- If you accept credit cards, show the appropriate emblems as visuals in your ad.
- Consider using color to demand attention.
- Promote any special services you offer, like the free rental of a spreader with the purchase of lawn fertilizer.

Other print ads

Other forms of print advertising include yearbooks, school programs and other "goodwill" promotions that can establish your name, make friends, and win customers. Be careful, however, that you don't exhaust your budget in the name of goodwill advertising.

Take to the airwaves

Broadcast advertising includes both radio and television commercials. Broadcast advertising usually requires a significant marketing budget, but the returns can also be significant.

Radio

Radio is a very effective medium for creating awareness. It reaches a wide audience and is often heard while driving, working, or during leisure time. It's very intrusive, effective, and actionable!

- Radio can often be targeted demographically (by age, location, etc.) and psychographically (types of music, lifestyles) so you can reach your target audience.

- Morning and evening drive times usually provide the most listeners, but they're also the most expensive times to advertise. They might not be the best slots for you.
- Ask if there's a garden or home show to sponsor. If not, suggest that you might host one. Nothing influences programming like a potential sponsor.
- Radio commercials can be prerecorded and sent to the station on tape, or you can ask station personalities to record your spots (this is usually cheaper, but you lose some creative control).

TV

Television advertising is a whole different ballgame, and a rather expensive one, so we'll cover it only briefly here.

- Commercials generally reach the widest audience in their homes.
- The expanding selection of cable channels is making television more accessible, even to smaller advertisers.
- The "information strip" that runs across the bottom of The Weather Channel is a good place to build awareness.
- If you can afford it, get on local gardening shows like those seen on HGTV.

One garden center does it all

Bordine Nursery, The Plant Place, in Rochester Hills, Michigan, is one of the nation's largest grower/retailers. According to Advertising Director Brenda Vaughn, Bordine's allocates 3.5 percent of sales to the company's marketing budget each year. Those dollars are then divided between print and broadcast advertising, sales promotions, special events such as open houses, and donations to local charities.

Because of their large marketing budget, Bordine's is able to run commercials on local radio and TV stations.

"Every spring, we sponsor a home gardening segment once a week on our local ABC-affiliate station," says Brenda. "We talk up new varieties and offer gardening tips, like fungal control. It's been wonderful for us. We see a spike in sales after every segment airs."

Get outside

Outdoor advertising offers great options to build awareness at a relatively low cost. The most popular outdoor advertising is the billboard. It lets you reach a mobile audience for an extended period of time—usually for one month or longer—depending on the contract you negotiate with your local outdoor company.

Other types of outdoor advertising include: signage on delivery vehicles, bus posters, subway car cards, taxi tops or trunks, airport terminals, telephone booth cards, and shopping mall kiosks or displays.

GrowerTalks, *February 1999.*

Budgeting for Your Marketing Plan

Mac Faulkner

There are two things to budget when you're developing a promotional campaign: money and time.

Time

The amount of time you'll need depends on how you decide to handle the creation and production of your marketing promotions. Some of the largest horticulture marketers employ a full-time creative and production staff. If you're doing it all yourself, you should plan to devote a significant amount of time to gathering information, developing your promotion, and scheduling media, especially when you're first starting out.

If you partner with seed companies for promotional help, you can save time by using some of the materials they've already produced. If you use tag companies as your creative resource, you get the benefit of working with marketing experts who already know the industry. Most provide their creative resources at very competitive rates.

If you hire a freelance writer/marketing consultant or an advertising agency, you'll likely spend a great deal of time meeting with them to teach them about your business. If the group you hire has previous industry experience, you'll get expertise well worth the time and money invested.

Money

There are two ways to determine a financial budget for your marketing and promotions: percent of sales and goal-oriented budgeting.

Percent of sales budgeting is exactly that—you allocate a certain percentage of annual sales for advertising. A good rule of thumb is 3 to 5 percent of your annual sales. A word of caution, however. If annual sales are down, that doesn't mean your advertising budget should go down, too. When sales are down, that's precisely when you need to advertise the most. Remember: Advertising is not a cost; it's an investment.

Goal-oriented budgeting is the allocation of a certain amount of funding to accomplish a specific promotional goal or event; for example, increased sales of vegetable plants in the spring.

Your accountant should be able to help you determine which method will work best for you. Your budget should be flexible enough to take advantage of unforeseen opportunities, but controlled enough so all your money isn't exhausted on goodwill ads.

Your location and your competitive environment govern your budget. The higher your visibility and traffic volume, the less you might need to budget. The more your competition is promoting themselves, the more you should be advertising.

However you decide to budget your funds, be sure to take advantage of industry resources, partnerships, and cooperative marketing efforts that can double your promotional power at a fraction of the cost.

GrowerTalks, *February 1999.*

Part 3:
Practical Ideas to Lure Customers
Mac Faulkner

It doesn't always cost a fortune to achieve success with promotional marketing efforts. Bordine Nursery, The Plant Place, in Rochester Hills, Michigan, gives its customers a coupon worth twenty-five cents toward the purchase of a poinsettia for each fifteen dollars' worth of goods they purchase during the year. That one little promotion keeps customers coming back all year.

"We've offered Poinsettia Money for many years now because our customers love it," explains Brenda Vaughn, Bordine's advertising director. Customers receive the cards when they shop from February through Thanksgiving. The coupons can be redeemed any time between Thanksgiving and Christmas Eve, but customers must also pay two dollars toward each poinsettia plant they buy with the coupons.

"It inspires them to come back and buy more of our products, all year round. It's our most successful promotion to date. We get 5 to 10 percent in redemptions every year," Brenda says.

Considering that 2 to 5 percent redemption is considered a successful response rate for most advertising and marketing promotions, Bordine's has obviously struck pay dirt with their Poinsettia Money.

Sales Promotion

Some people, even long-time marketers, get confused when we talk about sales promotion and merchandising. Many believe them to be the same. But there are subtle differences between the two, and knowing about these differences will enable you to allocate your marketing funds most appropriately.

Barron's Dictionary of Marketing Terms defines sales promotion as "activities, materials, devices and techniques used to supplement advertising and marketing efforts, and to help coordinate advertising with the personal selling effort." In other words, sales promotions are all of the combined activities, other than advertising, employed to sell a product or service. Among the most well-known sales promotion tools are:

- Coupons
- Promotional discounts
- Contests
- Sweepstakes
- Gift offers
- Special merchandising displays and materials

Merchandising is just one of the many tools within the sales promotion mix, and it's the horticulture marketer's most effective, easy-to-accomplish, and economical marketing tactic today.

Merchandising is defined by *Barron's* as "promotional sales activities of an advertiser's sales force, retailers, wholesalers or dealers, including point-of-purchase displays, guarantee seals, special sales and in-store promotions, designed to show a product or a service in a favorable light so that it will be purchased by the consuming public." In our industry, merchandising is managing and arranging merchandise on display in the store to promote sales.

Merchandising materials can be used to attract consumers to the retail outlet, lead them through the store, promote specific products, and prompt impulse purchases. Merchandising includes: banners, signs, posters, tags, and more. (See "Follow the Funnel" on p. 32.) These merchandising materials help businesses to differentiate themselves and their products, satisfy consumers' demands for more gardening information, provide a fun and convenient shopping experience, and help to ensure success with their plantings when consumers get home.

Banners, posters, signage, tags, literature racks, and more combine to create effective merchandising displays that attract customers.

Other helpful merchandising materials include literature racks full of planting tips and information about complementary plants and garden design. Also helpful is I.D. merchandise that features your business name, logo, phone number, and address. These items can include floor mats; smocks, shirts or jackets; plant packaging materials; or giveaway items like pens, garden stakes, mugs, or imprinted regional growing charts.

The ABCs of Direct Mail

For merchandising to be truly effective, you first need to get prospective customers into the store. Direct-mail marketing can help.

Direct mail is a marketing discipline unto itself with more guidelines and details than we have time or space to review here. Simply put, direct mail allows you to target and reach customers where they live or work, by age, gender, education levels, income, and more.

Direct mail is more accountable than general advertising because you can track your response rates and results. Direct mail fliers, catalogs, newsletters, tabloids, and postcards can be created to:

- Show and sell products
- Attract new customers and expand your selling base
- Upgrade current buyers
- Introduce new products
- Educate consumers
- Promote sales and special events

There are three basic elements you need to consider when using direct mail:

Lists

The most important ingredient in your direct mail promotion is the list of names you're mailing to. Your current customers, prospects identified by zip codes, and professionally compiled lists from list brokers should all be considered. You can buy lists of people who buy plants and gardening products through the mail. Just be sure that any list you use is current and contains only the types of people you want to attract as customers.

Products and promotions

The more compelling, clear, and concise your direct mail piece is, the more it will pull in customers. Show your products with attractive photography, and promote their benefits. Let your prospects know what's in it for them. A special offer or the word *free* will attract increased responses and improve the likelihood of customers calling, ordering, or visiting the retail outlet.

Timing

In most parts of the country, gardening product promotions are extremely time-sensitive. Be sure to plan ahead so your promotions hit your targets at the appropriate times. First-class mail will reach your target audience within two to three days, but it's the most expensive postage. Third-class bulk rate postage is about half the cost of first-class, but takes two to three weeks for delivery. When you have the time, plan ahead so you can mail at the lower bulk rates.

Spring Hill Nurseries in Tipp City, Ohio, does a good job with direct mail, using personalized imprinting on the cover and throughout its 1999 Spring Catalog. This attracts prospects' attention and makes them feel like the mailing was prepared especially for them. All featured products are guaranteed to grow in the region where the prospect lives. Inside, the reader is offered a free gift with any merchandise order of thirty dollars or more; double the free gift if orders are placed by a certain deadline. There's also a toll-free order number and a Web address for gardening tips and information. If there was a Siskel-and-Ebert team for direct-mail marketing, this catalog would receive "two green thumbs up!"

Untangling the Web

In recent years, the Internet has become a hotspot of information on virtually every topic in the world, and our industry needs to be there, too—providing planting, growing, and care information and suggesting new ways for even more consumers to use even more of our products.

But should we use the Web to sell? For all the benefits of cyberspace shopping (younger, more affluent buyers; low overhead; unlimited shelf space), there are also drawbacks. Many Web surfers remain non-shoppers. They're concerned about security and the ability of hackers to swipe credit card account numbers.

According to Jupiter Communications (*Newsweek,* Dec. 7, 1998), almost seventeen million people will buy something from a Web site in 1999. That's up from ten million last year and five million in 1996. The jury's still out on whether it will become a revenue source for our industry, but it certainly will be a growing center of information for our customers.

Spring Hill Nurseries joined with the National Gardening Association, Breck's of Holland, Stark Brothers, and Vermont Wildflower Farm to create and maintain www.gardensolutions.com. Brenda Vaughn says that Bordine's will have a Web site for their next catalog. "We want to establish a presence and see how it goes. I don't expect we'll see any big returns as yet."

PR and Publicity

Public relations and publicity are two important and relatively economical steps you can take to influence people's opinions and shape their attitudes about your business. Publicity is essentially "free" advertising when your news and activities are reported in the local and trade press.

By issuing press releases, you can gain:

- Prestige or a more favorable image
- Publicity for your products and services
- Good will from your customers, employees and suppliers as well as the industry
- Clarification of issues or misconceptions
- Public education about using your products

Special events are another way to create excitement about your business and products, win new customers, and expand your market. Some of these special events include:

- Open houses
- Care and planting workshops
- Live radio remote broadcasts from your business location
- Contests (such as a special giveaway during National Rose Month)
- Sponsoring a charity event or a community or sporting activity

Look for local publicity tie-ins, too, if you think they'll help you promote your business. These can include holiday parades; 4-H shows; state, county, or city fairs; garden shows; home/builders' shows; and business expos.

Promoting a special event adds notability and immediacy to your advertising efforts. And, to get the most bang for your buck, you can develop advertising based on the event or support your involvement with direct-mail promotions. Be sure to always post signs and fliers about your event where customers will see and respond to them.

Promotional Potpourri

Several other promotional marketing tactics are available to help you grow your business. These include:

- Business correspondence—Your letterhead, invoices, bills of lading, business cards, shipping labels, etc. should all reflect your business image and marketing slogan.
- Trade shows—We could write a book on this one. Look to your local library or the Internet for tips on how to make the most of trade show marketing and to follow up on the leads you generate.
- Co-op advertising—Many horticulture businesses are finding great rewards by partnering and sponsoring joint promotions with related or allied industry businesses. For example, Bonnie Plant Farms, Union Springs, Alabama, enjoys a successful co-marketing campaign with Miracle-Gro.
- On-hold messages—Make the most of the "dead" time when your customers are on hold. Use recordings to promote special sales, gardening tips, your Web site, or your value-added services.
- Frequent buyer programs—Bordine's Poinsettia Money is a prime example. Punch cards or certificates good for a certain amount off a purchase after meeting an established purchase amount can also keep customers coming back for more.

Obviously, time and money say you can't do all of these promotional tactics all of the time. But you can pick and choose among them to achieve your sales and business objectives.

Given your business plan for success, your desired image, your marketing budget, and your target audience, how can you ensure a successful return on your marketing investment? Next month, we'll show you how to "keep an eye on ROI" by reviewing the different ways you can track and analyze your marketing efforts.

GrowerTalks, *March 1999.*

Follow the Funnel

Mac Faulkner

If you think—and market—like today's gardening consumers shop, you can increase sales.

There are four basic steps to every sales process—attention, interest, conviction, and desire—and they all blend into something I call the "funnel approach." The "funnel" is a process consumers work through—whether consciously or subconsciously—before they make any purchase decisions.

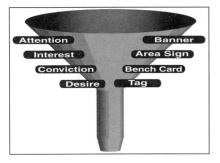

Using the funnel approach in horticulture marketing is actually a simple process and a sure way to increase sales.

First, you want to get Connie Consumer's attention as soon as possible. So, at the top of the funnel, a banner is hung outside your business location. The banner captures her attention as soon as she pulls into the parking lot or as she's driving by.

As Connie enters the store, the same marketing message is repeated using posters or area signs to build interest. As she moves into the area where product is merchandised, you move her further down the funnel with bench cards at the point of purchase to give her the information she requires—conviction that this is the right product for her.

Last, there's the product, which is tagged and merchandised creatively to convert her from a shopper into a buyer who desires your particular, hopefully branded, product.

If you're a sales-minded horticulture business, you're thinking like today's consumers. You're combining tags with other promotional materials—like posters, banners, signage, and merchandising displays—to meet consumers' needs for all types of information and to present a coordinated marketing effort and a professional business image. You're using these materials to effectively funnel customers through the purchase-decision process and helping them to make easy, quick, and informed buys—not just for a single plant but for the full and complete garden of their dreams.

Part 4:
How to Know Your Marketing Plan Worked

Mac Faulkner

As a horticulture business owner, you don't need to be a research whiz to know if your marketing has been successful. While entire companies exist to perform these necessary market research functions, in today's competitive business environment you should know enough about tracking and analyzing your marketing efforts to manage them sufficiently and to improve the effectiveness of future marketing plans.

At this point in our series, you've written and reviewed your business plan for success. You've honed in on your desired image and selected a marketing strategy to establish your point of distinction. You know your target audience and your budget, and you've created your promotional materials. Now, how can you measure the successful return on your marketing investment? Run the campaign. Monitor how it's implemented. And track the results.

Time Trials

It takes time and consistency to establish your image and build brand recognition with customers. A rule of thumb is that consumers must be exposed to your commercial message at least three times before they'll recognize it, recall it, and respond to it. One study on newspaper-advertising recall shows that you'll get the greatest response the seventh time a consumer sees your promotion.

The moral here is: Resist the urge to constantly change your advertising and core promotional message. It's important to make your brand consistent across all of your promotional materials, carrying out your message, your "look," and your themed approach on every tag, label, poster, sign, and catalog that you produce. You'll tire of your advertising materials long before today's media-bombarded consumers will.

Don't be too hasty to pull out of a campaign if you feel it isn't working as quickly or as well as you had initially hoped. There are always intangible benefits to having your good name and logo out there in front of consumers.

In fact, if you develop systems and methods to track and measure the results of your marketing promotions, you have a better chance of quantifying some of these intangible benefits of your campaign. This information can then be recycled as input for future promotional planning—and greater marketing success.

Tracking Methods

The easiest and cheapest way to track your marketing effectiveness is to carefully watch your floor traffic. Observe who's coming in and what's being purchased.

If you're a grower, spend time at your retail customers' businesses and observe these same things. Notice how people are reacting to your promotion versus a similar product or the same old varieties. Are your newly branded Merry Marigolds flying off the shelf? Are you seeing new and different types of customers? Become a keen-eyed market observer—enlist the help of everyone on your staff, especially delivery drivers because they are closest to what's going on at the customer level.

Another nonscientific yet effective way to monitor results is to simply ask customers, "How did you hear about us?" Keep a running record of their responses. Did they see your ad? Receive a mailing? Hear about you from a friend or business associate? The longer you run a themed campaign, the more you'll find that word of mouth can compound the effectiveness of your promotional investment.

A more reliable means of measuring response is to track sales of a given product at the beginning and end of your campaign. To see if you're attracting enough of the right kind of customers, ask for their zip codes at checkout. Zip code tracking will help you hone in on where your customers are coming from. It will also tell you which type of audience to focus on and where to mail the majority of your promotions if you're planning a direct-mail campaign.

Bordine Nursery, The Plant Place, Rochester Hills, Michigan, tracks zip codes at their cash registers. It helps them decide where and to whom their mailings should go. They send out seven newsletters each year to their in-house list of 30,000 customers. They also send their sixty-four-page, full-color catalog to 300,000 customers and prospects based on zip code targeting and analysis.

Other Tracking Methods

Direct mail tests

Rent a mailing list of potential customers from a professional list broker. Make sure the list matches, as closely as possible, all the age, income, and other demographic components of your current customer list. Or, to expand your market, select desired demographics for prospects you've targeted. Send one promotion to half the names on each list and another to the other half. See which promotion pulls the greatest response.

Telephone response

If you're advertising something special, such as a gardening guide, to customers who phone your business, list a different (false) name in the ad whom customers should ask for in each medium in which you're making the special offer. You'll be able to gauge which medium pulled best for you by tracking which name the majority of callers asked for.

Internet

If you've got a Web site, it's easy to track how many hits you get every day, month, or year. Some Web hosts can even measure the length of each visit. Remember, hits don't necessarily translate into sales. You can make your site more retail oriented and generate response by offering online coupons that visitors can download and print out. Or include a toll-free number they can call to order special merchandise, gardening guides, or other products.

Coupon clipping

Encoded couponing is another way to monitor response rates and track the effectiveness of your promotions. Coupons can take a variety of forms. Let's say you're promoting a summer special in three ways: a newspaper ad, a direct-mail flier, and a catalog you've created in partnership with one of your hard goods suppliers. Each promotional execution should show a coupon that has a small, different code at the bottom. When the coupons are redeemed, you'll be able to count them up and see which promotion pulled the greatest number of responses.

If you're running a print ad, ask the publication if they offer a split-run rate. Some newspapers and magazines will allow you to run separate ads in each half of the publication's circulation. This way, you can try two different offers at one time and see which one pulls in more customers. Keep running new ads against your "winning" ad, and then dump the loser to keep improving your promotional responses. Remember, words like *free* and *save* attract a lot of interest from consumers. Also, some folks respond when they see coupons, but they won't always cut them out and bring them in. Offer coupons at checkout, too, if that's how you're tracking sales of a specific product.

Inside its fall promotional circular, Plymouth Nursery and Garden Center, Plymouth, Michigan, included a simple brown bag. Customers were encouraged to "bring it in and fill it to the brim with an assortment of our cheery daffodil bulbs to plant now for spring." According to Steve Zoumbaris, garden center manager, the promotion "pulled good, but not great. We've done it for a few years now, and we'll probably do it again. Customers appreciate it. But we might offer one color next year, instead of the mixed varieties, so customers have an option and can be more selective in their plantings."

How Did You Measure Up?

At the end of your campaign, can you tell if sales increased as anticipated? Did you reach as many new prospects as you had originally planned? If you fell short of your goal, was there enough success to try it again? What parts of your promotion could you modify to improve the results even more?

Taking the time to evaluate what worked, what didn't, and how you might be able to improve results in the future provides valuable lessons that can be incorporated into your flexible business marketing plan.

Remember, marketing effectiveness isn't necessarily revealed by current sales and profit performance. Credibility and success are built over time. One of your results could be intangible image building, which will show a correlation to sales down the road.

There are many factors that should be reviewed on your marketing scorecard as you work your way toward maximizing every promotional dollar. These include:

- Operating efficiencies—Is there strong cooperation and a customer focus among all of your departments? Purchasing, production, sales, accounting and credit all need to be aware of and committed to your strategic marketing plans and implementation.
- Sales force coverage and involvement—Did you provide adequate information, incentives, and promotional supplies to carry out the mission you envisioned?
- Advertising and sales promotion methods—Did you make the right offer to the right audience? Did you tell them about it in the right way, at the right time, and through the right media? A brilliant strategic marketing plan counts for little if it's not implemented properly.

- Distribution channels—Did you have appropriate production, inventory controls, transportation, and delivery modes in place? Additional production and distribution capacities may be required to meet substantial sales increases.

Wrapping It Up

Sales increases are the most delightful results of the current national boom in gardening as a favored leisure-time activity. It's creating big profit opportunities for all of us and to capitalize on this trend we simply need to:

- Be different from the competition in our marketing efforts
- Reach consumers in ways that they're conditioned to respond
- Give them the information they want and must have before they buy
- Make them successful in their landscaping and gardening projects

As I've said before, we can't always be on the retail floor physically. And we can't be at consumers' homes when they're using our products. But with a well-developed and focused business plan—supported by appropriate and consistent marketing strategies and themed materials—we can most assuredly be with consumers when and where they're ready to buy.

And isn't that right where we want to be?

GrowerTalks, *April 1999.*

Keep Your Eye on ROI

Mac Faulkner

No one can guarantee what response rates you'll get from your marketing promotions because so many factors contribute to the outcome—your price, your competitor's price, timing, weather, and economic conditions, just to name a few. If you estimate the response rate required to meet your goals, however, you'll at least have a ballpark figure from which to work.

When you want to know if you are getting a reasonable return on your marketing investment (ROI), you can do it by finding your break-even point. Your break-even point represents the volume of inventory sales that will generate sufficient gross profit to cover your advertising expenses. At break-even, net profit will be zero.

To calculate your break-even sales volume, follow these steps:

1. Determine your average gross profit percentage:

Inventory sales	100%
Minus your average cost of goods sold %	-40%
Gross profit on inventory sales %	60%

2. Determine the sales volume necessary to cover advertising expenses:

Advertising expenses	$600
Times gross profit % (from step 1)	60%

$600 x 60% = $600 x .60 = $1,000 sales volume to break even

Here's an example: Your business has an opportunity to advertise in your community newspaper. The cost to create and run the ad is $1,200. What incremental sales dollars must be generated to justify the investment if the cost-of-goods-sold percentage of the advertised item is 38%?

1. Total expenditure = $1,200
2. Determine gross profit %:

Inventory sales	100%
Minus cost of goods sold %	-38%
Gross profit on inventory sales %	62%

3. Divide total expenditures (step 1) by gross profit % (step 2):

$1,200 x .62 = $1,935

You'll need to generate $1,935 in sales directly from the ad to break even on your advertising investment. If you feel you'll get this level of response, then go for it!

GrowerTalks, *April 1999.*

Keep Your Advertising Legal

Mac Faulkner

When you're creating new marketing or advertising material, it's important that what you present is truthful. Misleading advertising can create unhappy customers and, on rare occasions, legal action. Laws differ in every state, and you should always consult an attorney when legal advice is required.

Here are five main areas to consider in developing your advertising and marketing promotions:

Rights of privacy—Don't use people's names or pictures in an advertisement or flier without having their consent in writing ahead of time.

Rights of ownership—Don't use any ideas, quotes, photographs, artwork, music, motion pictures, or sound recordings that are under copyright by another person. The shortest copyrights exceed fifty years, and some exceed 100 years. If you use testimonials from customers or suppliers, always make sure you have their prior consent and that you attribute the comments to them.

Rights of competitors—Never run any advertising with the intent to discredit your competition. If you make any comparisons, make sure they can be substantiated by an independent source.

Rights of consumers—Be certain that your advertising is clear enough to offer only one interpretation to the average reader. Make sure any prices you give are clearly explained and reflect exactly what is pictured. And be sure you can meet any promises you make, including available stock of sale merchandise.

Contest rules—Laws differ in every state. In most cases, states bar you from holding a lottery, which is gambling. If you want to run a contest, your safest bet is to clear everything in advance with your attorney.

Obviously, this is very general information and not a substitute for legal advice. If you have any doubts about the legality of your advertising or promotional materials, consult legal counsel.

GrowerTalks, *April 1999.*

Chapter 3

To Marketing We Will Go:
Marketing & Promotions

Warm and Fuzzy Feeling

Dave Hamlen

Recently at a local pet store I talked to a mother and her young daughter. The mother said she shops there because a portion of each sale is donated to the Humane Society. The daughter enjoys the store because there's a petting area for children. Both mother and daughter shop there because it conveys a caring image. People are attracted more toward a business that displays a concern for good rather than one that appears to be lining its pockets.

Here in Vermont, Ben and Jerry's Ice Cream has built that kind of image. They donate ice cream to help organizations raise money for worthy causes. This generosity has helped them to grow from a store located in a converted gas station to a multimillion-dollar company.

Donations for Improved Image

One retailer I know has developed a program called Partners in Patronage. An organization requests a donation on a card, and each person from that organization can bring the card to the retailer's store. When the card is presented at the register, a percentage of the sale is credited to the organization. Giving donations to groups or organizations is a good way to express your compassionate business nature. If possible, get the donation mentioned in your local paper or your newsletter or post pictures at your business.

Donations don't always have to be monetary. They can be gifts of time. You and your employees can teach children how to plant a flowerbed at their local school, or you can man the phones at a public television fund-raiser or give blood to the Red Cross.

Computer companies have found that donating products to schools is valuable to their company image. Not only do they get their product in the hands of future users, but local taxpayers also look on it favorably.

Attract Young and Old

Each of us has a wonderful opportunity—and perhaps an obligation—to educate future gardeners. Promote a caring image by talking at schools, Girl or Boy Scouts, 4-H groups, and organizations with potential future gardeners.

Give your time to establish a kids' garden club to help create future gardeners and bring in parents who garden. Parents appreciate your investment in educating their children. A kids' garden club is also a way of getting some of your own planting done. Our kids' garden club grew tomatoes and gave them to a soup kitchen to help feed the homeless.

Intergenerational gardening is also becoming popular. When young people work with senior citizens, satisfying results can occur. When you help sponsor intergenerational gardening, you not only help people feel productive, but you help meet a basic human need—feeling wanted.

Gifts and Discounts Are Appreciated

Another way to attract kids to gardening is to give them a monthly gift. At our garden center, we call this our plant-a-seed project. Each child up to age sixteen is eligible to receive a card with his or her name on it along with the months of the year. Every month that the child comes in—usually accompanied by an adult—the card is punched, and the child receives a free gift. Gifts may be a seed packet, pots, dried flowers, a plant, potting soil, or holiday decorations.

Discounts to senior citizens, groups, or organizations will also make your business more attractive. People like to think they're special and that you appreciate them. A discount to a specific group helps convey that feeling.

Customers also appreciate sales, promotions, and buyers clubs. The occasional sale or specially priced items are messages to customers saying, "I want your business."

Price Competitively When You Can

Another way to give the impression of being an empathetic business is to be competitively priced. Pick competitive items that tend to be price sensitive and then meet that price or create a loss leader to help dispel the illusion that you're expensive. A word of caution: You don't have a large chain store's buying power. You can competitively price a few items, but don't try to butt heads with the discount stores. Customers should be attracted by your business's professionalism, not just price.

Remember to have plenty of information available to help your customers become successful gardeners. This will help make you an expert and create repeat business.

Giving a warm and fuzzy impression can do a lot for your business image. People will support you because they feel you're supporting them.

GrowerTalks, *Point of Sale, July 1994.*

Wild and Crazy Promotions

Dave Hamlen

Do you want your business to be noticed? Do you want to attract more customers than you currently do? Then wild and crazy promotions may be for you.

In North Branford, Connecticut, the Van Wilgens want to make their garden center a fun place to shop. The first weekend in May, the Van Wilgens hire a helicopter for the day to give free five-minute rides. This promotion packed their parking lot for the entire day.

The first weekend in June, the Van Wilgens hold an herb and art weekend. They invite area artists to paint at their garden center. Along with the artists, they have herb seminars and specials on roses, annuals, and nursery plants. They also offer herbal teas, herb recipes, and dried herb arrangements while a flute player entertains. To announce this promotion, Linda Van Wilgen mails a flyer to forty thousand people, and it is mentioned in their newsletter and the newspaper.

In the fall, the Van Wilgens hold an Octoberfest with a German band, German food, and a pumpkin hunt. When children find a pumpkin, they get to keep it and also receive a prize.

Linda has also joined together with other area businesses to offer a trip to Hawaii through a local radio station. Because the garden center purchased a certain amount of radio advertising, Van Wilgen's customers who signed up got a chance at the trip.

Jim Bergantz of Bergantz Nursery in Angels Camp, California, needed to stretch his advertising dollars. To do this, Bergantz teamed up with two other retailers. The trio tripled their advertising power and sales. One year later, their cooperative advertising includes twenty other retailers. The businesses call themselves NAME (North Angels Merchants Extraordinaire).

One promotion that has worked well for NAME is called "Paint the Town Red." In late December, NAME mails out three thousand seed packets. These packets contain seeds of red flowering plants. By the end of April, the town is a blaze of red color, which coincides with their "Paint the Town Red" weekend.

Along with red flowers, the town sees red costumes, red flags, and red vintage cars. Events like a pancake breakfast, sun-up cattle drive, street dance, barbecue, fine arts show, classic red car show, live music, theater, telling of the town's past, and activities like blacksmithing and panning for gold make it a fun weekend for all who attend. While visitors see all this red, Bergantz and the other merchants of NAME see a lot of green from this promotion.

Unusual promotions are not uncommon to Waterloo Gardens in Exton, Pennsylvania. In October, Waterloo Gardens has a Halloween contest. Their employees set up haunting displays in the greenhouses, nursery, and store. Customers are given score cards to rate the various displays. The winning displays are given cash prizes. It's a great way to have customers see more products while having fun.

They hold a similar contest for container gardens. Employees are allowed to use any materials available at Waterloo for the containers. Customers judge the container gardens, and cash prizes are awarded to employees. As a result, Waterloo customers are exposed to some very creative container gardening.

In Swanton, Vermont, where my garden center is located, it was rumored for several months that the Grateful Dead was coming to play. For a town with a population of 2,500 people, this was big news. Why a small town in northern Vermont? It seems the Dead had a problem getting into Canada. They wanted to give a concert for their Canadian fans, so they chose northern Vermont.

You could feel the excitement. An audience of 60,000 to 100,000 people was projected. I tried to figure how we could take advantage of this situation, and the answer was a dead plant sale.

To emphasize the sale, ten days before the event we put up a three-by-seven-foot banner on a sales shed near the road. The banner said, "Dead Plant Sale" with a picture of Jerry Garcia. I felt this would either go over well or I would start reading the employment ads.

Fortunately, it worked. Our local newspaper and radio station noticed the banner and mentioned it. Business for that month increased 26 percent. Six weeks after the banner came down, people were still talking about it. The only advertising cost was one birdbath (wholesale value less than ten dollars), which is what the person who drew the banner wanted for doing it. It was a very profitable promotion, even if we didn't sell one dead plant.

Unconventional promotions attract customers. Doing something unusual and fun sets you apart from other retailers. You can also team up with other businesses in your community for additional advertising strength.

Remember that when it comes to promotions, the wilder and crazier the promotion, the more you will be noticed. But they're not for the weak or squeamish retailer. Promotions may not get you a place in the *Guinness Book of World Records,* but if done properly, they will get you noticed.

GrowerTalks, *Point of Sale, April 1995.*

Garden Center Festivals: Worth All That Work

Margaret K. Kelly

People dressing up as Easter bunnies, bobbing for apples, going on hayrides—is this horticulture? Not exactly, but it certainly is marketing. Getting customers to come to your location and getting them to know your business is just part of what garden center festivals are all about.

For five years, Hicks Nurseries in Westbury, New York, on Long Island has been starting off the season with their Spring Flower Show and Garden Expo. This huge event gets both Hicks' customers and employees excited about the growing season. Held the third weekend in March, it gets people thinking about and planning their gardens.

The gardens that Hicks features range from a children's garden complete with a morning glory scarecrow, a rose garden, a spring bulb garden to a vegetable garden with bean plants ready for harvest. The pizza garden captured people's imagination by having all the necessary ingredients to top a pizza—tomatoes, oregano, parsley, peppers, and onions—in a relatively small area. When kids asked their parents if they could grow that at their house, the parents could confidently answer yes.

A complete house front built on the Benjamin Moore Paint/Goldsmith Seeds color promotion shows color coordinating plants as part of a patio display. They also showcased Fantasy petunias from Goldsmith due to be available in 1996, which shows their customers that Hicks is out looking for new plants.

Customers can find an array of activities. Seminars are presented each hour from 9 A.M. to 4 P.M. featuring Hicks staff, supplier representatives, and local television and newspaper gardening experts. In the floral department, customers find ongoing flower arranging demonstrations. Children find hands-on planting activities. To keep families at the festival through mealtime, a café offers hot dogs, hot pretzels, cappuccino, and cookies.

The Garden Show excites people with flowers, Fred Hicks says. It helps him compete with the mass merchants since this is something mass merchants can't do, and it helps the public understand how Hicks Nurseries is different.

Logistics begin far in advance of the time Hicks designs the gardens. They force all their own material since they have the greenhouse space and can maintain control.

Getting the Most from Your Efforts

Once you've done all that initial work, be sure to get the most from it. If you're going to do a one-day event, you might as well make it two days. Hicks is well tuned into this—sponsoring a pre-opening reception to which they invite community leaders, their good customers, suppliers, and the press. Along with enjoying some wine and cheese, these people get a peek at the show before it is open to the public.

This spring Hicks extended their show into a second weekend, thus keeping gardens open for a full week plus two weekends. The second weekend they invited horticulture associations ranging from the Orchid Society, the Rhododendron Society, area garden clubs, and the Hemerocallis Society. They gave the second weekend a different name—a Horticultural Fair—and offered seminars by association members.

Fabulous Fall

In the fall, a sense of excitement—perhaps even frenzy—cranks up at Martin Viette's Nurseries in East Norwich, New York. In an effort to extend the season, Martin Viette's has been conducting their Fall Harvest Festival for eighteen years. The festival grew slowly from pumpkin and mum sales to what is now a different event every weekend after Labor Day until Halloween.

What does Viette's offer? There are pumpkin sales with pumpkin painting and a giant pumpkin weight contest. Families compete in a family scarecrow contest. Apple sales have exploded. Hayrides are drawn by horses and "antique" tractors. There is a huge craft fair where vendors set up their own booths to sell their wares. A live bluegrass band provides background music every weekend. They have a petting zoo and large costumed characters to greet children. Garden club members receive fall specials—last year it was blue hollies at half price.

In fact, Viette's fall festival has gotten so big that one weekend last year they had more than eight hundred cars, which forced them to close the front gates for a half-an-hour until traffic subsided. After many, many years of conducting their Fall Festival and building traffic, Russell Ireland, president of Martin Viette's, says they are now looking to refine and streamline their efforts. Viette's knows they can get large numbers of people to come to their garden center—now they want to get the right people and the right product mix. Viette's is refocusing efforts on how to get the people to come in and buy items with the best return.

So Why Do a Festival?

Many growers and garden center retailers turn to festivals to extend the season—either to get customers in earlier in the spring or later in the fall. Festivals generate traffic and get people into your business: And they let people know what your business is all about. Once the consumer is in your store, you can demonstrate your knowledge of horticulture and the personal service you provide.

GrowerTalks, *July 1995.*

ABCs of Festival Success

Margaret K. Kelly

Advertising. Do enough and target it so people know about your event. Consider bag stuffers, newsletters, newspapers, radio and TV. Invite your local TV newscaster or meteorologist to broadcast from your site.

Families. Keep it family oriented and the numbers will be amazing. Have hands-on activities for children and a place to sit for grandparents.

Food. When people get hungry they will eat. If you don't have food they will leave. Lack of bathrooms is another reason people leave stores.

Garbage. If it's as big as you'd like, there will be garbage. Have extra cans out to handle it. Have staff ready to pick up garbage on the ground.

Image. Remember who you are and think about how you are perceived. Russ Ireland cautions if you're not careful it can get to be a circus, and you have to decide if that's the image you want to project.

Other events. Check the holiday and community calendar to be sure you are not conflicting with another popular event.

Parking. Martin Viette's uses 12 trained parking attendants working with radios to maximize space and minimize congestion.

Review. Be sure to discuss the entire event with staff. What went well—what didn't? Can you change things Saturday night to make Sunday better?

Seminars. Holding seminars during a festival, or anytime, helps to project your store as a source of gardening information. Expertise sells—promote it!

Traffic flow. Be ready to handle the number of people you have. Direct them through your store and to the festival events. Use signs and maps where necessary.

GrowerTalks, *July 1995.*

Stick-to-it-iveness

Stan Pohmer

There's no lack of great ideas forthcoming from suppliers and retailers of horticultural products: new concepts for products and merchandising, new marketing themes, new displays and presentations, new POS/POP programs, new advertising strategies—all very exciting and adventuresome.

We are, however, an industry that is a little short on patience. We're looking for that instantaneous positive customer and consumer response, that instant gratification, and, as a result, we may be selling our programs and ourselves a little short. Any new concept or program needs some time to be recognized, tried, and experienced to take root and start producing positive results. Consumers don't quickly recognize change or accept it readily . . . they're creatures of habit, and they fall into the rut of complacency. That's not to say that they don't like or appreciate newness; it just takes time for them to get used to the new ideas and then start reacting positively to them with their spending.

Because of this, we need to be consistent in our approach and give these new ideas a chance to take hold. Too often we put a new product or program in place and, when we don't see the immediate results that we expected, we condemn it, throw it out, revise it too severely, and come to the sometimes erroneous conclusion that the concept is wrong or just won't work. We then go on to developing the replacement strategy and start the process all over again.

The reality is that sometimes we just aren't giving the new program a chance to become recognized and established. The consumer just sees "burn and churn"—constant change—and perceives low strength of conviction from the producer or retailer to what they feel is a good idea.

Why Do We Fail?

Maybe we introduced a new product and the weather was bad. Maybe we introduced a new advertising campaign and a competitor ran a strong ad at the same time. Maybe we introduced a new POS/POP program and we're not hearing the positive feedback from the consumer because they aren't having the problems they've had in the past (consumers are quick to tell us what they don't like but are much slower in giving us positive feedback). Maybe the idea is sound, but it isn't instantly effective because of outside influences and reasons. Maybe we just need to give it a little more time and keep supporting it to generate the results we expected.

That's not to say that all new ideas will work. We need to continually evaluate them and weed out the ones that are flawed, but consider the reasons that they aren't successful. Perhaps all it will take to turn it around is a little fine-tuning, a little more support, and a little more time.

If you truly believed in the new strategy when you proposed it, chances are it is a good idea. Have a little strength of conviction, a little patience, some stick-to-it-iveness, and give it a chance to succeed.

Pohmer's Perspective, January/February 1999.

Focus Your Promotion

Chris Beytes

How does a young independent garden center in only its third spring in business and surrounded by established, high-quality competitors boost its sales 140 percent compared with last year? Advertising and promotion, that's how. Of course, it doesn't hurt that the owner has thirty years of experience in marketing for corporate America.

Roger Yost, who retires this month as chief marketing strategist for apparel manufacturer Jantzen Inc., is building a new career—that of garden center retailer. Owner of the Wine Country Nursery, Newbery, Oregon, Roger says a major part of his strategy involves advertising. In fact, he's investing about 12 percent of his sales towards making Wine Country a recognized brand name in the Portland area.

"Because we're new, we spend a disproportionate amount on advertising and promotion," Roger admits. "I don't recommend that people do what I do." At 12 percent, he's well above the average that he says most companies spend on advertising and promotion, which is 2 to 5 percent of gross.

But it's paid off: In just three years of advertising on television, in newspapers, and through direct mail, Roger saw his sales increase 36 percent last year (from what he calls a "modest" base). This year he was hoping for a 30 percent increase, and so far he's running 140 percent above last year. And that's in a market that's well stocked with top-notch independent garden centers and some pretty good chains, such as Eagle Hardware. How much of that growth does Roger attribute to his marketing strategy?

"A whole lot," he replies. "We knew that it would be a disproportionately high investment, but on the other hand, having seen the results of new product launches in the past, I saw no other way to do it. We were either going to be a player, or we're out of it."

With thirty-plus years of marketing experience, Roger knows how to reach and influence potential customers. "The consumer is a very sophisticated individual right now," he says. "They know value when they see it, they know quality when they see it, they love honesty and refreshing invitations. Some time ago, even ten years ago, there wasn't enough information for them to make decisions. [Today] they know what they're looking for when they come in."

So how does Roger invest his advertising dollars? With what he calls a "360-degree marketing effort" composed of television ads, direct mail, and weekly newspaper ads. Here's how he makes his strategy work.

Television

Roger is "heavily" into television, sponsoring local gardening expert Ed Hume's syndicated gardening show, along with "Rebecca's Garden," another syndicated show. He also buys time on Home and Garden Television (HGTV) in the Portland market. His ads run every other week during the spring, once an hour, all day long. Sponsoring major shows and advertising on a network such as HGTV makes Wine Country "somewhat larger than life," Roger says. Viewers don't realize he's only buying advertising for a small portion of one market the cable shows reach.

He rotates three or four different ads that promote different aspects of Wine Country. With twenty-five years of experience producing television ads, Roger has learned that the human eye and mind can absorb quick shifts in imagery. "Sometimes ads dwell too long on a particular topic or picture," he says. His ads use a "rapid fire" approach, but with a "warm verbal invitation" and "pleasant imagery" that dwell not only on plants, but also on the way Wine Country presents bulbs, dry goods, pots, and other products.

Two keys to television success are consistency and variety. He runs three or four different ads to keep viewers from getting bored. But he makes sure each ad is consistent in its look and that viewers know who's doing the advertising. "We push our logo very hard, both as sign-on and sign-off, and mention verbally the name Wine Country at least four to five times in a half-minute spot," Roger says. "We emphasize that because we are a brand, and we're competing with other garden centers that have been here much longer and that provide very good service."

Print Ads

"There is a fashion to the garden center business, and I came out of the fashion industry," Roger says of his advertising focus. He says that today's consumers are attracted by the unusual, by messages that go beyond price and selection, which he calls "the prices of admission for an all-purpose garden center."

"What we try to do, both in our commercials and our print ads, is to put a twist or turn on a particular plant or shrub," Roger says. For instance, Wine Country specializes in unusual Chinese trees and shrubs, so he focuses on that aspect of his business. Another of their specialties is water gardening. Many nurseries carry pond supplies, but Wine Country emphasizes that they are aquatic consultants and suppliers to the Washington Park Zoo, which gives an expert image and sets them apart. "It's an expression of what's new and different," Roger says of his ad focus.

Image, either good or bad, is created in your ads and in the venues you choose. For instance, hard lines such as fertilizer are pretty boring to show in ads. Roger chooses vendors who not only have good products, but who have bright, colorful, eye-catching packaging. "When we put these in our commercials, there's the illusion of excitement even in the dry goods area," Roger says.

The focus of your ads determines your image, too. If you focus on price, that's all customers will associate with your business. Roger says that sales or special prices are fine, but should be used sparingly to build traffic or at the end of the season.

As for venues, advertising in shoppers or classified ad-type publications only furthers the low-price image. He chooses community newspapers, which efficiently target local customers. And selected ads, whether they are gardening publications or television shows, target "serious" customers. "That's why Revlon and other cosmetic companies [advertise] in beauty magazines," he says.

Direct Mail

The final third of Roger's promotional strategy is direct mail, which he uses to target new homeowners, an expanding demographic base in Portland. Using an Oakland, California, direct-mail company, he sends out 280 to 300 pieces per month from March through June to new move-ins, offering a special no-restrictions discount. The flier also describes all of the products they carry, rather than just saying, "Come in and get 20 percent off." "That's been one of the most valuable forms of communication that we've done," he says, adding that the average sale has been around a hundred dollars and that most have turned into repeat customers.

Hints

"There's a cacophony of information that a lot of ads I see are providing," Roger says. "Too often, unfortunately, it's price based." If that's your biggest selling point, then that's what you promote. But if price isn't the image you want, don't push it just because your competitors are. In fact, Roger says he looks at competitors' ads to see if they're pushing any common products through co-op ad deals. If so, he avoids promoting that same product.

Standing out from the competition applies not only to your business, but also to your advertising. You should treat promotion not as a necessary evil, but as a way to grow your business and to establish your name and your place in the market. Says Roger: "This is investment spending to me. We are a brand."

Consumer Buzz, May/June 1998.

TV: Are You Where Your Customers Are?

Have you taken your company's message to the television screen yet? Maybe now's the time: Everything about television viewership is on the increase, including the number of TVs, the number of viewers, the number of channels, and the amount of time spent watching, according to a survey conducted by Media Dynamics and reported in *Research ALERT*. But be forewarned: The audience you reach depends on many factors.

Statistics from the survey include the number of hours per day the average household TV is on (seven), the number of channels the average adult watches in a week (nine), and the average number of hours spent in front of the TV per day (four).

Who's doing all the watching? Media Dynamics broke their survey down into those people who are most likely to be heavy users and those most likely to be light users. Heavy users include: mothers with babies and large families who are most likely to be home most of the day; older, retired adults; homebodies; homemakers; and the unemployed. Light users include: students with full school days, socially active people, sports enthusiasts, persons with demanding jobs who often work late, and persons with full-time jobs. The survey also reveals that people with "more discriminating tastes" are liable to be light viewers, as are "those affluent enough to engage in many entertaining or informative pastimes." Heavy viewers are characterized as having "less sophisticated tastes" and as "tired, overburdened persons who use TV as a relaxant," among other characteristics.

Does this mean you shouldn't advertise on TV? Not at all. You just need to consider your channel choices based on the customers you're trying to reach. For instance, more affluent households (over $60,000 per year) are more likely to watch PBS and pay cable stations than those households earning under $39,000 per year. Conversely, average- and lower-income households watch more network, local, and independent stations.

Consumer Buzz, July/August 1998.

How Important Are Brands? Very!

Brand recognition is on the rise in America, pushing generics and private labels to the back of the shelf, according to the 1997 Yankelovich MONITOR Survey, as reported by *Marketing Tools* magazine.

Their survey shows that a known/trusted brand name is a "strong influence" on purchase decisions for 63 percent of respondents, compared with 51 percent in 1994. Statistics regarding brands increased across the board since 1994, including the statements: "Some makes are worth paying more for" and "Once I find a brand that satisfies me, I usually don't experiment with new ones."

Marketing News says that name recognition has become so valuable an asset "that some companies have outsourced the actual manufacturing process so they can devote all their attention to nurturing the brand." Examples include Nike, which doesn't own sneaker manufacturing facilities; and Sara Lee, which owns Champion, Playtex, Hanes, and Hillshire Farms, but which has been selling its bakeries, textile, and meat-processing plants. Just how much can a brand be worth? *Financial World* magazine estimated Coca-Cola's brand name at $39 billion in 1985.

Brands will continue to increase in importance, according to Don Schultz, author of *Measuring Brand Communication Return on Investment.* *Marketing Tools* quotes him as saying, "Twenty-first century organizations have to compete on brands because they have nothing left. They can't get product differentiation, they can't get superior pricing, distribution, or promotion, so branding strategy is it."

Consumer Buzz, May/June 1998.

Why National Brands Bring Top Dollar

Perceived quality is the main reason consumers will pay more for a national brand than a store brand or private label, but how much more they'll pay heavily depends on the product category, according to research conducted by the Marketing Science Institute and reported in *Research ALERT.*

Consumers rated twenty product categories, such as aluminum foil, bleach, cheese, soft drinks, and toilet tissue, according to how much quality difference they perceived between store brands and national brands and how much of a price premium they were willing to pay. Roughly 40 percent of consumers see store brands as equal or superior to national brands, but less than 10 percent are willing to pay equal or higher prices for the store brand. The average perceived quality difference for the twenty categories was 20 percent, and the average price premium they're willing to pay is 35 percent.

Here are a few interesting statistics about national brands:

- Consumers won't pay as high a premium for a national brand on products costing less than three dollars.
- Consumers are less willing to pay premium prices for staple products they frequently purchase.
- Good news for floral brands: Consumers say they're willing to pay a higher premium for products that are associated with pleasure (such as flowers and plants), compared with products that are considered "functional" (such as aluminum foil).

Of the 20 products surveyed, which category had the highest perceived value for national brands, and which were consumers willing to pay the highest premium for? Dog food, at 49 percent and 45.5 percent, respectively.

Consumer Buzz, July/August 1998.

Marketing versus Selling

Stan Pohmer

Competition for both retailers and suppliers is getting more intense every day. Not only are consumers faced with more choices than ever before, but the number of storefronts merchandising floral and lawn-and-garden products is growing at a far faster rate than the growth in the population, which makes protecting market share more difficult. If we keep doing the same things we've been doing, we'll lose the battle for consumers' dollars; the status quo can no longer maintain equilibrium.

I recently read a review of *From Mind to Marketing*, by Dr. Roger D. Blackwell, professor of marketing, The Ohio State University, and president of his own consulting firm. The book deals with the demand chain, focusing on consumers and how they use products: "The consumer's mind is where it all begins."

One of the key points I took away from this review was his perspective on the difference between selling and marketing. From Dr. Blackwell's viewpoint, the process of selling is getting rid of what a retailer owns or a company produces (what one of my friends in the horticulture industry aptly calls "eradicating the inventory"); the process of marketing is getting a company to make, and the retailer to carry, what it can sell.

I've always believed that the most successful players in our industry, both suppliers and retailers, are those who take the marketing approach rather than the selling approach in operating their businesses. Sure, retailers make bad buys (items and quantities), and suppliers produce the wrong items, or, if you're in the Sunbelt markets, El Niño weather patterns play havoc with consumer demand, and selling through the inventory ownership takes precedence over marketing. But these should be exceptions to the rule rather than the way we do business on a regular basis.

Weather being the major exception, if we identify what consumers really want, need, and expect, then build our items, programs, and promotional/merchandising activities to support them, we should expect to see higher sales, higher inventory turnover, less need to give product away, and lower shrink/dump as benefits to suppliers and retailers. And if we're really doing these things to address consumer needs, then we should also see higher consumer satisfaction levels. This will be the key factor in increasing consumption and building market share for our industry on a short- and long-term basis.

Every retail operation has its own specific customer base, focusing on different demographics and different merchandising and promotional positions. It takes hard work and a lot of analysis to get the right products in the right stores at the right time to support consumers, but these marketing activities are what retailing is fundamentally all about. This marketing process should include the suppliers; with their expertise added, the timing can be accelerated and the benefits can be shared.

Perhaps we should consider changing the titles from buyers and salesmen to marketers to better reflect the real focus of what retailers and suppliers should be doing to compete in today's marketplace.

Pohmer's Perspective, May/June 1998.

To Sell, You Must Tell

Chris Beytes

Earlier this year I wrote a column in sister publication *GrowerTalks* suggesting to the flower breeding companies that because POP material is now so important, they should develop colorful, flashy tags first, then breed flowers to go with them.

I was only half kidding—my suggestion came after seeing several very interesting new bedding plants with unusual habits, growth characteristics, or potential uses. Breeders, naturally, are quick to point out these novel traits to their customers—mainly seed and plant distributors. Distributors will, no doubt, pass most of that information along to growers. And we in the media do what we can to keep our readers informed of what's new and different.

My concern is for what happens next: Will the growers from whom you buy tell you about these new varieties' novel characteristics? And most important, will you educate your customers? All too often, the answer is no. Somewhere in the chain, a fascinating plant turns into just one more pack or pot left to languish on the retail shelf next to its "ordinary" cousins.

Two Sides of the Coin

When the miniature-flowered Fantasy petunia series was unveiled in 1995 by Goldsmith Seeds, we in the industry knew it was a hit from the beginning, and we took it for granted that gardeners would instinctively know what to do with it. "It's so great, it will sell itself," seemed to be the marketing cry.

Unfortunately, it's a safe bet that few garden consumers, even hardcore enthusiasts, know about Fantasy, at least based on the marketing efforts I've seen at retail. For every good display of Fantasy, I've seen twenty places where it's simply been put on the shelf next to the large-flowered petunias. In that situation, consumers see it not as a cute little petunia that's great for containers or for edging a walkway, but as a runt.

England took a different tack with Fantasies. Colegrave Seeds, which distributes Fantasy in the U.K., was very clear on how to market it: for baskets, bowls, and containers. They even gave it an expanded name: "Fantasy, the Junior Petunia," to help tell consumers about this new petunia. They left nothing to chance, and sales, while not blistering, have reflected the success of that strategy.

Another Goldsmith variety, Mosaic impatiens, shows the other side of the coin. Industry experts think it looks like it either has a virus or thrips because of its unusual, striped flowers. And yet the general public loves it.

Obviously, the key to a new variety's success has little to do with industry "experts" and everything to do with the end consumer. If a variety's unique traits are readily apparent, such as with Mosaic, then it should sell itself. If uniqueness lies not in something obvious like flower color, then we have to do everything possible to make consumers aware of that trait.

There are at least a dozen new bedding plants for '99 that could languish on your shelves if you don't make it your business to learn everything that makes them special, then share that information with your customers.

In My Opinion, November/December 1998.

Perennial Retailers Are "Selling a Promise"

While the annual Perennial Plant Association (PPA) Symposium most often focuses on production methods, more and more of the talks and tours focus on marketing. This year's conference, held in Boston, Massachusetts, July 6-11, was no exception.

The most common and valuable point made by all the speakers was that when you sell plants, particularly perennials, you're selling a promise, a hope of what that plant is going to be as it grows. Your job as a retailer is to help your customers visualize that end result.

Show Customers What They're Getting

Highly recommended is the use of large picture tags. The new locking tags are especially good in conjunction with a pot designed to lock it into place. These new tags stay in place throughout the marketing chain and don't end up scattered on the ground at your garden center after a busy day of customers handling them.

Ian Baldwin, who consults and lectures worldwide on the topic of marketing plants, recommends that retailers create display gardens within their garden centers. If space is a premium, use what he terms "mannequins"—"Set up a great looking sample of the crop on sale that has been forced into color so people can see what they will get from that little green scraggly thing potted up on the bench," he told attendees.

Other ideas from Ian include using endcaps as mini display areas, growing larger size product, providing better training for your employees on product knowledge, using plant cards to inform customers, and making a concerted effort to seek out new plants.

Quick, Functional, Fun

The consumers with the greatest amount of disposable income drive buying trends in perennials.

"Typically, the largest purchasers of gardening materials are those in the forty- to sixty-year-old group," says Steve Frowine, president of The Great Plant Company, New Hartford, Connecticut.

The baby boomers have reached that age group now and will continue to have the greatest influence over sales in the general marketplace, Steve pointed out in his talk. "The things we're discovering about them and their shopping patterns indicate that they are discriminating, well-educated people with more disposable income who are often stressed, in a hurry, and have less free time," he said. What that translates into for the retailer is a need to provide the information a customer requires to come to a clear decision quickly. And as Ian Baldwin noted, personal satisfaction has become a major factor in today's consumers. You're not going to succeed unless your product is "quick, functional, or fun."

Eye Level, September/October 1998.

Chapter 4
The Internet: Out of Site!

Making Money on the Internet:
Tips for Successful Web Profits

Douglas C. Green

Let's be clear right from the start: The vast majority of the more than 375 million Web pages out there don't make money. While Yahoo has declared a small profit, most Internet stars such as Amazon.com and Netscape have yet to show a penny of profit. Instead, they're sinkholes into which investors are pouring incredible amounts of money. However, profits are possible.

John Shelley of John Shelley's Garden Center, Felton, Pennsylvania, in a speech to the Southeast Greenhouse Conference and Trade Show (SGCTS) said, "In '96, I did $86,300 from Internet business. In '97, just over $136,000 came in as a direct result of the Web site. This year, we'll probably do close to $200,000 in additional business. Roughly 80 percent of these figures are from landscape contracting, 15 percent from retail sales, and 5 percent walk-in from out-of-state people 'finding' us and coming to visit. I'm still amazed, as I sit and go over the day's requests, at just how many people from somewhere else want our expertise, based upon what they've experienced at my corporate site."

Paul Begick of Begick's Nursery and Garden Center, Bay City, Michigan, on the other hand, says of his site: "I frankly don't know. We don't sell 'directly' off the site. My original intention for the site was to make our products and services known to people in our shopping area (a thirty- to fifty-mile radius) who like to browse the Web sites. At this time not enough people have commented about our site to know whether or not it was a worthwhile investment."

These comments really beg two questions: Can you make money on the Web? And what's the rush to have your own company Web page if it's not certain you'll make money? The answers are as deceptively simple as they are expensive. Making money depends both on the product and marketing, just as in non-Web operation. Companies are rushing to the Net because it's there, because it might mean profits in the future, and most important, because their competitors are there. Here are some guidelines for developing Web pages that might make it easier to succeed.

Set Objectives

The first thing to understand about a Web page is that it's part of your business and represents an investment of time and resources. Like any other part of your business, the site should have clear objectives and fit within the business planning and profit objective methods your company uses. The objectives for a Web page have to be clear and measurable because without a measure of objective worth, the site all too easily becomes ineffective, consuming company resources instead of contributing to the bottom line. Web sites are fun to play with, absorb incredible amounts of time, energy, and resources, but they usually contribute very little to a greenhouse company's profits. For example, one small group of Web owners and newsletter publishers estimated they spent a minimum of eight hours a week on their sites and newsletters and weren't yet profitable. This means 20 percent of their labor went into an unprofitable venture.

Because the site design follows directly from the objectives, the site will reflect the quality of those objectives. At the very least, the site plan should clearly outline three things. The first describes the intended visitor—in other words, who or what group is the intended site audience. Second, outline the content of the site: What's the site providing to its visitors, and what's it selling? Last, but not least, the site's computer architecture and software needs must be set. For example, if there's going to be online shopping at the site, the software will be drastically different from non-shopping sites. These objectives can be measured and tracked, and the site can be modified accordingly.

Understand that the Net is international. At our operation, Simple Gifts Farm in Athens, Ontario, Canada, we started our Web page as a support service for our local greenhouse customers. Within six months of running the site, we discovered the vast majority of our visitors weren't greenhouse customers. There weren't enough local visitors to justify the site's ongoing expenses, even though we'd done extensive advertising in the newspapers, in the greenhouse sales area, and in print newsletters. Our initial objective of supporting local plant sales was shelved, and the only reason the site still exists (and is being redesigned) is that we have a new business and a new business plan that it will support.

Graph It out First

The best advice I received when doing my site design was to do it on paper first. While most designers use a tree-form layout, I found a spider web, or circular form, works better for me. The home or index page is set in the center of the circle and the next layer of main pages is grouped around the index page. The internal links to these main pages are easily drawn to connect this main framework. Each main page then supports its own circle of supporting pages.

With these circular drawings, the necessary internal links become apparent. Revisions or additions are made, and links are drawn as needed. These drawings then become work lists when the electronic Web designs are coded; they can also be used as checklists. My drawings now are full of working notes and check marks as I hook up all of the necessary links to make the pages work together.

Content Is King

"Content is king" is the Internet marketer's mantra. A collection of pretty pictures might be interesting for a one-time visit, and a simple business description might occasion a short visit—but to keep visitors coming back, to get your page bookmarked, you have to provide content. Visitors have to get information from your site that's fresh and updated regularly. The best sites are updated daily or weekly, and the sites you visit only once are static displays.

Not only is content king, but the content has to be freely given away. There are so many competing sites where content is freely given that your greenhouse site has virtually no chance of selling any information at all. Whatever the sales objective, remember that information is the most important thing you're providing, and this information has to be free to the customer. Visitors will come back for this information and then, once they begin to trust you, you'll have the chance to sell your product. Internet research also suggests that a sales pitch dressed up as content is worthless and soon avoided by visitors. You can see through disguised sales pitches, and so can your visitors.

Don't Be Fancy: KISS

Just because it can be done electronically doesn't mean it should be done. The first time I see a graphic scrolling across the page it's interesting; the tenth time I quickly hit the back button. The most feared script I now see is

"Starting Java" because I know it's going to eat up time and will rarely give me something useful. Fancy graphics and lengthy download times only guarantee high reject rates by visitors. Some data suggest users will only wait a few seconds to see if your page loads correctly, and the average time spent per page is less than twenty seconds.

Most experienced Internet users surf with their graphics turned off, so don't be swayed by the Internet designer who wants to put the "cool" graphics on your page. Follow the old KISS rule: Keep It Simple, Stupid. Graphics do have their place, and once you start using them, run each one through one of the freely available graphic optimization programs to decrease download time. Similarly, avoid wallpaper and black backgrounds, and keep frames out of the design at all costs, as most search engines do not like them.

Black text is read easily by all browsers. Go to another color at your own peril, because what shows up on your design screen isn't necessarily what shows up on the Internet for other browsers. If your customer base is older than twenty-five years, use larger text and avoid light-colored text, such as yellow, because older eyes don't work as well as they used to.

Have a simple objective for each page, using as little memory per page as you can. Even if you have a direct cable line, many browsers are still powered by slower 14.4 modems and will back-click if the page loads too slowly. Avoid lengthy download times like the plague. Do visit some of the Internet design Web sites; they regularly have pages describing how to design good sites and pitfalls to avoid.

Do It Yourself or Spend Big Bucks?

Your Web pages are the face you put on your business. Just as your advertising and company premises exemplify who you are, so do your Web pages. If first impressions count, then this is your electronic first impression. If you don't understand Web page design, and you want to run shopping carts to sell online plants (as a wholesaler or retailer), then you'd better have a good designer set up the software and site architecture.

On the other hand, there is Web design software that's easily learned and will do a basic job with a short learning curve. Beginner HTML programs are freely available on the Net through Microsoft, Netscape, and other sources using the search directions in the accompanying sidebar. Having the work done commercially is easier on the nerves but harder on the checkbook. Page design and implementation cost between fifty to two hundred dollars per page, depending on the complexity of the page and site. If you do the work internally or if your company assumes maintenance duties of an outside-designed site, give one person responsibility for the site, allowing peripheral help from others; otherwise, the pages will quickly resemble the back bench of an old greenhouse, complete with attendant garbage.

The Web isn't going away; economic forecasters unanimously agree that it'll become a vital part of twenty-first-century business. The question isn't why or how you'll get onto the Net—the question really is when will you do so.

GrowerTalks, *January 1999.*

How to Search the Web

Douglas C. Green

Finding things on the Web is easy; finding useful things on the Web is a bit tougher. All search engines have two different options for searching—the normal and the enhanced, or pro, level. I do the vast majority of my searching at the normal level, but I do use several tricks of the trade to increase the likelihood of finding something useful.

To begin with, I check my spelling of the word I want to find. While some Web sites actually enter wrong spellings as part of their meta tags (and get good hits due to search typing errors), correct spelling will help more often than not. For example, "gardening" is more useful than "gardning," but both will get you information.

Secondly, if the data I'm searching for is a two-word concept, such as a name or a specific term like *garden center,* then I enclose that term with quotation marks to tell the search engine program I want both words to be treated as a single word. For example, I entered the term *garden center* without quotation marks at www.hotbot.com and got 148,539 results back. I received their lists of those who had *garden* and/or those who had *center* as part of the site. As soon as I put quotation marks around the words, I reduced that number to 6,755. Still a large number, but the results were now more focused.

To further shrink the search, use a plus sign (+) between terms. To search for garden centers with perennials, I used the format "garden center" + "perennials" and received 785 replies. To further cut these responses to something useful, I added a geographic location, so the information request now looks like "garden center" + "perennials" + "New York." HotBot returned 114 garden centers in New York that listed perennials. While I wouldn't go to all of their sites, certainly the first two or three pages of the listing had enough information to keep me busy for some time.

As a last note, there are major differences between search engines in their structure and formats. For example, Yahoo isn't a search engine; it's more properly referred to as a review site (now changing itself to a Web portal, or entry point). It doesn't search the Internet but reviews and lists sites for folks to use. Search engines have different strengths and information based on the computer algorithms used to find information. It's necessary to experiment with the over two hundred different engines to discover which work the best and provide the best information for you and your needs.

Recent research indicates using search engines is the No. 1 activity of those browsing the Web. Now, for first prize, tell me the most searched-for information. Clue: three-letter word ending in the letter *x*.

Here's a very useful address for search engine descriptions: http://www.writerswrite.com/journal/may98/gak5.htm. Although aimed at writers, it's one of the best introductions and includes descriptions of the biggest and most-used search engines.

GrowerTalks, *January 1999.*

Knowing Online Lingo Keeps Customers Happy

Douglas C. Green

If you have a Web page or are thinking of joining the Web revolution, understanding Web culture is important. Gardeners are quite gentle and forgiving when compared with some other users of the Internet. Yet while you may understand how to communicate with customers when they're in your greenhouses, there are different customs and cultures on the Internet.

You ignore these customs at your peril because Net users respond quickly (and sometimes furiously) to real or imagined slights. On the marketing mailing lists, there are constant conversations about customers who write nasty letters to business operations and those businesses' Internet Service Providers (ISPs), sometimes causing the ISPs to cancel Internet operations for the businesses. A classic case is the customer who asks to be added to a newsletter list and then forgets that he requested this newsletter. When the newsletter arrives, he think it's spam (unrequested e-mail), complains to the ISP, and the ISP cancels the company Internet access—all without the company knowing what has happened. Be aware of the Internet and its customs.

You also need to have a good working relationship with your ISP. Make sure they know what policies exist at your site. As in the greenhouse industry, a little attention to small details will stop big problems from reaching out with their nasty surprises. What follows are a few hints to help your Web operations run more smoothly.

Make Sure You're Understood

Some people write their e-mail with the keyboard CAPS LOCK KEY TURNED ON. Using capitals is the equivalent of shouting on the Internet, and, while you may find using the caps lock key useful when e-mailing your mother-in-law, it grates on the nerves of experienced e-mailers. To smooth ruffled feathers, try using emoticons. These little symbols— :-) happy, :-(sad, ;-) wry grin—are quite useful at defusing emotionless monitor printing.

Because the printed word can be easily misinterpreted, especially by customers with a problem, using these emoticons to show your good intent will defuse potential problems. Consider the sentence: "There's a problem here." Now put each of the three emoticons after that sentence to affect the meaning. Which meaning do you want to send to your customers? Knowing customers as you do :-), you know they'll pick the meaning that you did not intend :-(, and then you have problems ;-). You can download hundreds of emoticons at www.utopiasw.demon.co.uk/, if you're interested in communicating without words.

Instant Gratification or Else

The Internet is a fast medium compared with the postal service. Customers who use your e-mail service or the Contact Us button on your Web page expect you to respond immediately. If you don't, you create the image of not caring about them.

Same-day or, at the latest, next-day responses, even if only to say you're working on their problem, are the standard of performance in business communication on the Web. Avoid creating a situation like one of the responses I received when doing research for this article. I visited a greenhouse site that said, "Click here with a question." I did and received an e-mail from the ISP (non-greenhouse) Webmaster saying, "Here's an 800 number to call with your question." The 800 number didn't work in my area code.

Business is lost in small ways like this. In visiting commercial sites that serve the industry, I found sites without customer response buttons; sites that didn't respond to my requests for information (what kind of business would not respond to a writer's request and the potential for free publicity?); and the site of one of my suppliers that demanded an entrance code. Separating the wholesale customers from non-wholesale trade is fine; however, this supplier never told me about the entrance code. My immediate response was to ask myself why I wasn't a good enough customer to get an entrance code.

If you do something on your site to exclude some visitors, ensure that the site is publicized to the industry or supply a method to allow new customers access to your site. That is, of course, unless new customers aren't important to your business ;-).

Maintain, Maintain, Maintain

One small way in which customers are lost to your site is the dreaded 404 message that informs them that a link on your site is not working. To prevent this, you must maintain, maintain, maintain. If you think watching a flower crop for pests demands concentration, you haven't tried to maintain a large Internet site.

Once your site is operational, go to an Internet-accessible computer at a friend's house and find your site. Explore the site, use all the links, and see how long it takes the pictures to download. Perform all of this checking away from the computer that created the site, and you might find a few unpleasant surprises.

An acquaintance's Web site was in operation for more than six months before I visited it and discovered that all the pages were straight black with no writing. For six months his site had been full of black pages (he was using black backgrounds), and nobody had told him the site was not operational.

Delegate one person to be in charge of your site. This ensures the consistency of the site and leaves someone with the responsibility of doing all the necessary work. It's the same as greenhouse work: Unless it's part of the job to find pests, nobody is going to look because finding some only creates more work. Unless it's part of the job to find Web page bugs, nobody will look.

Keep It Fresh

A static Web page is a dead Web page. Unless the pages are updated regularly, your visitors will stay away in droves. Although they'll only spend an average of twenty seconds per page when they visit, visitors have to have a reason to come back. As a businessperson, you want all the twenty-second visits you can get. You do this by regularly giving them something new. This can be new pictures, new product updates, information from publications (ask permission first), a special of the week—anything to change the site.

Community Spirit

Creating a community is the new goal of Web page marketers. By doing this, a core group of customers can be maintained for less cost than more traditional methods. This group can be used for research, marketing, and evaluation. The easiest way to create a community is by using opt-in newsletters, or listserv-type mailing lists. (See next article.)

Creating the community is hard work, but it's another potential source of income from the Web. For example, we ran a plant special this past spring that was advertised only to our newsletter list. To get the plant at the special price, the customer had to identify himself as a newsletter recipient. The day after we sent out the notice of the special, those plants sold out.

The Internet isn't a foreign country, but it might as well be. If you learn the customs, learn the language, and learn the ways of doing things, you can have a successful experience in this electronic world. Translate those successful experiences to your customers, and you might find them willing to travel with you, bringing some of their money with them.

GrowerTalks, *March 1999.*

Customer Newsletters: Next Killer App?

Douglas C. Green

E-mail is a killer app. Killer apps are those computer programs or applications that make it useful, all by themselves, to own a computer. Just as the spreadsheet program Visicalc was the first killer app, e-mail is now one of the best reasons to own a networked computer. While Visicalc crunched numbers, e-mail crunches distance.

Business owners are flocking to e-mail with astounding speed. It's a communication device that helps create a community around a particular product, person, or activity. A community on the Internet is much like a community in a geographic setting: Both share a similar range of ideas and interests. On the Internet, that sharing of ideas and interests is particularly well segmented, with mailing lists and interest groups springing up to share every conceivable interest.

Webmasters can take advantage of this by sending newsletters to a customer base. There are

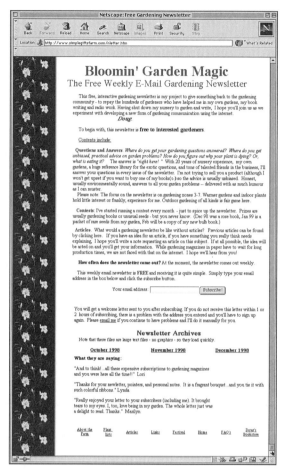

several aspects of a successful newsletter that help in creating and expanding an Internet community. To begin with, the newsletter is about news; it's not about selling product. A gardening newsletter has to be about gardening and good gardening tips, not full of sales information. A retailing newsletter put out by a wholesaler has to be about retailing tips. To be sure, readers tolerate some business stuff, but for the most part your community doesn't exist to be sold to—it exists to be informed.

A newsletter is about creating trust. Once those in your community trust you to give them useful data, they'll be more inclined to purchase a product when you suggest it as a solution.

A newsletter is about being personal. The best newsletters share something of their author's personality. In creating community and trust, the author has to be known to the readers.

Newsletters should be "opt-in." This means that the letter is sent only to those who request it through your Web site. Don't mass mail using e-mail. Mass mailing is called spamming, and it will only do you harm on the Internet. In some states, such as Washington, spamming is illegal and will quickly attract problems and fines. Spammers are the bane of the Internet and if your business is identified as a spammer, you'll find it easier to fix a dead furnace on a zero-degree night than to deal with all the nasty letters you and your ISP will receive.

Editor's note: For a sample or a subscription of Simple Gifts Farm's newsletter, go to http://www.simplegiftsfarm.com/nletter.htm.

GrowerTalks, *March 1999.*

Chapter 5
Nothing but the Plants

Long-Lasting Bromeliads

Laurie Beytes

Bromeliads are one flowering pot plant that all retailers should stock in their stores. Why? "Shelf life, shelf life, shelf life," says Kerry Herndon of Kerry's Bromeliad Nursery, Homestead, Florida.

Kerry is one of the pioneers of the bromeliad market in the U.S. and has been selling bromeliads for twenty-two years. He grows about 1.5 million pots annually. His bromeliad sales are increasing every year, and *Guzmania* is now the most popular. Kerry says that's because *Guzmania* offers a wide range of flower colors, including red, orange, yellow, and purple and has soft, green foliage. He adds that breeders are hard at work developing even more *Guzmania* colors, especially pinks.

Aechmea fasciata, or silver vase, used to be the No. 1 seller for Kerry and is still "a classic, wonderful plant," he says. With its large, silver-green leaves and majestic pink flower spike, it's a great choice.

Vriesia is also popular. It typically has medium green foliage (sometimes with stripes) and red or red-and-yellow flowers that tend to be shaped somewhat like a sword, hence the plant's common name, flaming sword. Kerry says to watch for a new class of green-leafed *Vriesia* with "absolutely spectacular" flowers that should soon be coming to market.

Which varieties should you carry? That depends on the nature of your business. Because bromeliads come in such a wide range of shapes, sizes, and price points, there is something for every retailer, from four-inch plastic pots for $2.25 to large specimen plants in fancy upgraded containers for $25 wholesale. In addition to offering a wide selection to your customers, consider trying a mass display. Kerry says he's repeatedly seen the success of a large display of just one variety in one color—it makes a big impact.

What's the No. 1 problem at store level? According to Kerry, it's complete lack of water. While this affects bromeliads less than other potted plants, it can still shorten their shelf life. He recommends keeping the soil moist, as

well as putting a little water among the lower leaves. Excess water in the center cup can cause the plant to rot and damage the flower. Changing the cup water and misting the foliage can also help prolong the life of your plant.

Bromeliads used to be sold as hobbyists' plants to be kept year after year, but according to Kerry, most customers today enjoy them for the several months that they're in bloom, then discard them. However, anybody can continue to enjoy their bromeliads after they bloom. While the "mother" plant will die after blooming, it will produce "pups" that grow from its base. These pups can be carefully cut from the mother plant and put into their own pots to grow and bloom.

"Summertime is a very popular time of year for grocery chains to carry bromeliads, when they need a flowering item that has long shelf life," he says. Bromeliads can easily last three weeks to a month in your store, giving every retailer plenty of opportunity to sell them during the dog days of summer. A wide range of varieties, long shelf life, and reasonable prices make bromeliads a perfect plant for your customers' home decor. That's why Kerry calls them "the best houseplants that exist."

Live Focus, July/August 1998.

Choosing the Perfect Pot Mum

Laurie Beytes

With so many different colors and flower forms available, it's no wonder that the chrysanthemum is still the No.1 year-round produced pot plant in the industry. Hundreds of cultivars are available, and new ones are being created all the time. Here are some tips to help you, the retailer, make sure you're getting the highest quality pot mums for your customers.

Greenhouses that specialize in growing pot mums aren't just looking at color and flower form. Take into consideration the number of weeks a variety takes to flower. A shorter "response time" may allow a few more plants to be produced for you each season. Think about how vigorously a variety grows. This has bearing on the duration of lighting and the amount of growth retardant used, which can add or subtract from the cost of producing that variety. Another important factor to consider, and the one that would most pertain to the quality of the plants you buy, is the season of best perform-

ance. Some varieties are durable enough to be considered appropriate for growing year-round, which could be in the summertime heat of Orlando, Florida, or the low-light and cooler wintertime of Minneapolis, Minnesota. Others require the "perfect environment" to be produced, so they'll have a limited range of suitable production months. This is why some varieties seem to be available only at certain times of the year.

To make sure you're getting the best quality pot mums for your customers, look for the following characteristics:

For a 6½-inch pot
A sturdy plant that has good proportion in relation to the size of its pot.
- Total plant height of fourteen to eighteen inches and width of at least fourteen inches across the top of the flowers.
- At least fifteen single flowers or thirty-seven multiple flowers per pot, with a nice "tabletop" effect.
- Flowers that are a third to half open for multiple flowered types like daisies and half to three-quarters open for single-flowered types like decoratives.
- Foliage that has a fresh appearance and a nice green color, with no blemishes of any kind.

For a 4-inch pot
Look for the same characteristics as above, except that the total plant height will be nine to twelve inches, and the width will be at least seven inches across the top of the flowers. Also, you'll be looking for at least four flowers open or almost open, with a uniform distribution of flower buds.

Live Focus, November/December 1997.

Cyclamen: Elegance in a Pot

Laurie Beytes

The next time a customer asks you to recommend a nice pot plant, tell them to try a cyclamen. The florists' cyclamen (*Cyclamen persicum*) is native to the Mediterranean, and when it comes to longevity in pot plants, they're hard to beat! Not only are they available in shades of pink, purple, salmon, red, and white, but they also come with single, double, or fringed flower forms, and their flowers are sometimes scented. There are three basic plant/flower sizes: minis, which are usually offered in four-inch pots; intermediate sizes (midis), which are typically found in five-inch pots; and standard types (large-flowered), which are usually offered in six-inch pots. Some even have beautiful variegated foliage. And they can last for several months with just a little care.

Cyclamen really prefer bright light without direct sun, but they'll tolerate a little direct morning sun as long as they remain fairly cool. They grow best

in temperatures between 55 and 65°F. If they're getting an adequate amount of light, then you'll find that they continue to produce flower buds and blooms and will provide the long-lasting color display. Growing from tubers, cyclamen don't like to be kept soggy or left standing in water, but they don't want to be completely dry either. Keep them lightly moist, and they'll continue to reward you for months to come!

Live Focus, September/October 1998.

Impatiens versus Impatiens

Laurie Beytes

It may not be the War of the Roses, but it's really a tough decision for many garden center customers. The decision of course, is whether to purchase standard impatiens or New Guinea impatiens. Both are in big demand, so be prepared to offer your customers some good advice.

Impatiens

Impatiens walleriana, sometimes called Sultana impatiens, are native to Africa (Kenya, Malawi, and Mozambique). They were first introduced in the U.S. in 1965 and are the No. 1 bedding plant produced from seed in the U.S. today, with 15.5 million flats produced in 1996.

Impatiens are noted for being a great choice for flowers to grow in the shade. Most often found in packs, they make fantastic flowerbeds but can also be used in hanging baskets, window boxes, color bowls, etc. They come in a huge range of colors, pastel and vivid, as well as "star" types that are striped with white, "swirl" types whose petals fade from a darker edge to a

lighter center, and the
new "mosaic" types
that have a streaked
effect. And there are
also those with varie-
gated foliage. Breeders
have really given us
an awesome selection
from which to choose.

New Guinea Impatiens

New Guinea impatiens, *Impatiens hawkeri,* is native to the subtropical high-
lands of the South Pacific. It was first introduced in the U.S. in 1972, and
today's varieties are definitely more desirable due to breeding improvements.
Growth habits are more uniform, and plants have more flowers held nicely
above the canopy of the foliage.

New Guinea impatiens tend to be marketed more as the Cadillac of impatiens, being larger plants with larger flowers and leaves than *Impatiens
walleriana.* They're typically found less often in packs but rather in four-inch
or six-inch pots or hanging baskets, and they're often used as the "feature"
plant in combination planters.

While they can be
used in beds, they're
easiest to care for when
grown in containers
where soil moisture
can be monitored
more easily. Being
from the rainforest,
New Guinea impatiens
prefer to grow in an
evenly moist soil at all times. They come in many beautiful colors, and some
of their flowers are bicolor and have a fluorescent quality. Whether with
green or variegated foliage, they create a stunning display.

While they may take some morning sun, both impatiens and New
Guinea impatiens prefer bright light with no direct sun, especially if the
temperature is above 80°F. Keep in mind that the more sun they're in, the
more water and fertilizer they'll require.

So how do you decide which impatiens to recommend? The amount of time and money a customer is able or willing to spend for a particular purpose will probably be the determining factor. So offer some good suggestions, and when the smoke clears, chances are pretty good that you'll have sold one or the other.

Live Focus, May/June 1998.

Bring the Outdoors in with Ivy

Laurie Beytes

The word *hedera* is Latin for ivy. And the genus *Hedera* may only include a few species, but it has literally hundreds of varieties. These are woody-stemmed climbing plants with beautiful, leathery leaves, and they're some of the most versatile plants on the market today. But where should your customers use them?

Indoors

Hedera species are terrific houseplants to use in hanging baskets, to soften the interior decor as they cascade off of the edges of windowsills, mantels, and tables, or as a common component in dish gardens. And *Hedera* spp. are quite the rage these days when they're trained into topiaries. These elegant forms give your customers another way to bring the outdoors in, a popular theme in decorating right now. And if elegant isn't what you're looking for, how about a topiary animal—there is a virtual zoo to choose from.

Outdoors

Hedera is also great for using outdoors, depending on what species you use. *Hedera helix* (common English ivy) is the hardiest species, good for planting in Zones 5 to 9. *Hedera colchica* (Persian ivy) is hardy in Zones 6 to 9. And *Hedera canariensis* (Algerian ivy) is hardy in Zones 7 to 10. No matter which zone you live in, *Hedera* can be used seasonally in window boxes, color bowls, hanging planters, and beds. Whether you use it alone or incorporate it with your annuals or other plants, just remember that *Hedera* is usually best in the shade (bright light without direct sun).

Care and Handling

While most species of *Hedera* require only bright light, in the case of variegated varieties, two or three hours of direct sunlight a day may be necessary. Plants will become spindly if they don't receive adequate light. And although they'll tolerate a wide range of temperatures, around 50°F is ideal.

Water *Hedera* moderately, allowing the top of the soil to dry out between waterings. And be aware that they definitely don't like to be left sitting in water. They do, however, like frequent showers, which not only help to provide them with some humidity but also help to discourage spider mites, ivies' most common pest problem.

Because *Hedera* species are such versatile plants, they should be available to consumers in a wide array of sizes: from plugs that can be used by customers who would like to create their own topiaries, to one-gallon pots for the landscape, to eight-inch or ten-inch hanging baskets that can be moved to wherever your customer needs them. Inspire your customers by also offering a good representative sample of the huge variety of leaf shapes and colors that are available.

Live Focus, September/October 1998.

Orchids: Easy Color for Any Gardener

Laurie Beytes

Orchids can be found worldwide, except in the major deserts and the Arctic Circle. The diversity in their flowers and even the plants themselves are almost as vast as their range of native habitats. Certainly there's an orchid to please everyone. In fact, many orchids are quite easy to grow and actually make wonderful houseplants! Here are a few recommendations.

Moth Orchid

Phalaenopsis hybrids are among the most popular orchids on the market today, and they're some of the easiest orchids for customers to grow. This is due in part to the fact that they grow so well under the low-light conditions that are often found in most people's homes and also because they flower for months at a time. *Phalaenopsis* produce a spike of flowers that can last from two to five months, and they can even flower twice a year. Flowers come in white as well as many shades of pink, lavender, peach, and yellow. They often have stripes  or speckles. The plant itself has long, broad leaves that can be either medium green or mottled with grayish green and may have a purple underside. Native to the tropics of Asia, they prefer to be kept moist, with bright light or morning sun.

Lady Slipper Orchid

Paphiopedilum spp. and their hybrids are also very easy orchids to grow and make a great choice for a windowsill plant. They fall into two broad categories: those native to the high mountains where the climate is cool and moist, and those that dwell on the warm forest floors. Members of the first group have grassy green foliage, usually bloom in the winter, and prefer to be grown cool. Those in the second group have handsome mottled leaves, generally bloom in the summer, and prefer to be grown a little warmer. *Paphiopedilum* flowers in striking, often bizarre, color combinations—background colors may be white, yellow, green, or a combination thereof, with markings in tan, mahogany brown, maroon, green, or white.

Nun's Orchid

Phaius tankervilliae is a medium-green, upright-growing orchid with long, pleated leaves. It's native to China and Australia. It produces tall flower spikes with ten to fifteen flowers each. Blooms are white on the back and reddish brown inside, with a lip that has a yellow throat. The flowers appear in late winter or early spring. Nun's orchids are vigorous growers and require plenty of water; just be sure that they also have very good drainage. They grow best in very bright light or in morning sun.

Jewel Orchid

Ludisia discolor is native to Burma and has beautiful velvet-brown leaves with reddish stripes and reddish undersides. The spikes of white flowers emerge during winter, and each floret has a striking yellow anther. Jewel orchids like to be kept moist but not soggy and prefer to grow in very bright light with no direct sunlight.

Special thanks to: Dana Harrison, Orchids by Hausermann, Villa Park, Illinois.
Live Focus, March/April 1999.

Dish Gardens: Not Just for Florists

Laurie Beytes

Traditional dish gardens aren't just for florists anymore; they're something that all plant retailers should consider carrying. Their great gift appeal and easy maintenance requirements should make them a staple item.

Traditional dish gardens are typically made up of a variety of foliage plants, suitable for interior light levels, which are attractively arranged in a basket, ceramic bowl, or other container. There are a few variations on this theme that you might also want to consider.

This cactus dish garden adds a South-western flavor to any location.

European dish gardens are a fancier version of the traditional dish garden in that they also contain a blooming plant. These are especially popular for holidays such as Mother's Day. Cactus gardens offer a different twist by featuring cactus or succulents, generally displayed in a Southwestern theme. This makes them great for full-sun locations such as a deck. And bromeliad gardens, whether artfully displayed on driftwood or in a more traditional container, have an exotic presence all their own!

Live Focus, July/August 1998.

Nursery Stock Comes of Age

Chris Beytes

Ten years ago, if you'd asked a typical garden consumer what a topiary is, she might not have known.

Today, thanks to Martha Stewart, Home & Garden TV (HGTV), and the myriad of consumer gardening magazines, that same consumer not only is likely to know what a topiary is, she may even have one planted near her front door as the focal point of her landscape. Or she may be a fan of exotic dwarf conifers, bonsai, "multigeneric constructs," Japanese maples, or any number of unusual trees and shrubs.

While Martha and others can take credit for exposing garden consumers to these new plant forms, much of the credit must go to the nursery industry, which has brought topiary and some formerly exotic plants out of the world's botanical gardens and into the North American landscape.

However, topiaries are just one visible indication of the level of sophistication that the nursery industry has reached in response to widespread changes both in retailers' needs and consumers' desires. Nursery growers will tell you that growing a quality product is no longer their only focus, as it was for the previous generation. That important task now has to share top billing with customer service, marketing, and running a stable, competitive business. And, like other segments of horticulture, the nursery industry is even considering end consumers' desires.

To learn more about the nursery industry, we visited three innovative Northwestern nurseries: Iseli Nursery in Boring, Oregon; Monrovia Nursery, with locations in Azusa and Visalia, California, and Dayton, Oregon (we toured the Dayton location); and Briggs Nursery, Olympia, Washington. During our visits, we found some excellent examples of the innovations coming from tree and shrub growers.

The Space Squeeze

In the "old days," retailers would place their tree and shrub orders for the year and take one or two large deliveries early in the season. Plants would be stored in the back of the garden center until needed, where they'd slowly languish. Or they'd be shoved together into one area of the garden center, often times not properly tagged or priced. Either way, valuable retail space was wasted, and good quality plants soon became unsalable.

Retailers today can't settle for that if they want to turn a profit. "A lot of our customers have restructured their businesses to make them more of a destination," explains Fran McFarland, marketing manager for Briggs Nursery. "They might have put in a display garden, maybe a water feature . . . so they don't have as much room to have all those plants in there. They don't want the big shipments anymore. They want to place a big order, then take it in little bits and pieces."

In response, growers have adapted their shipping schedules to offer smaller, more frequent shipments, which has both its good side and its bad side. To the good, plant quality is now higher at many garden centers because they're turning over the stock faster and bringing in fresh stock more often. The downside is that regional growers now have an edge over growers who've developed a niche delivering nationwide. For years, large nurseries like Monrovia have shipped across the country with impunity because they faced little competition. Today, however, especially east of the Mississippi, more growers are able to grow high-quality plants that can be delivered faster and more cost-effectively than those from the West Coast can.

Rick Wells, general manager of Monrovia's Oregon location, says Monrovia's biggest competition comes from regional growers who can serve a small area very well. Monrovia's solution will likely be to develop East Coast and Midwest locations, according to Pam Wasson, director of marketing, either by aligning with other growers or by buying other growers.

For Iseli Nursery, consolidation may be the key: They were purchased by International Garden Products, which also bought bedding plant and perennial producer Skagit Gardens, Mount Vernon, Washington. Container rose grower Weeks Roses was also purchased by IGP soon after. This partnership could allow Iseli, Skagit, and Weeks to expand their services and offerings to customers.

Information, Please

Another challenge to growers is POP. No longer is it enough to grow the plant and hang a generic tag from a branch. Nurseries are asking for more assistance in selling their trees and shrubs, which helps them shorten the time that product sits in their garden centers. POP has become almost a standard item in the bedding plant segment of the industry; tree and shrub growers are being forced to follow suit.

For example, you may have noticed how much better many companies' tags are. Monrovia recently redesigned its logo and tags to be more appealing to consumers, especially women. André Iseli says his company is also focused on giving not only better information to retailers and consumers, but on presenting it in clearer, easier-to-understand ways. "We're measurably enhancing the descriptive adjectives of how to grow a plant, how to take care of it, how the garden center should take care of that material, because shelf life is so important," he says. "We're trying to do everything we can to enhance the ability of garden centers to sell our product."

Monrovia wants to help garden centers sell their products by developing a consumer brand. To that end, they recently dropped "Nursery Company" from their logo, changed the logo from "MN" in a yellow-and-black oval to a wood-print-style flower, and added the tagline "Horticultural craftsmen since 1926" to "elevate the status of plants," says Pam, and to let consumers know that the company has a long history. They'll also double the amount of advertising in consumer magazines and on HGTV, which they tested this spring. Fran says Briggs is also looking at ways to expand their company's name, initially through a new Web site.

Briggs and Monrovia have both set up formal ways to get feedback from retailers—Briggs through a focus group and Monrovia through regional retail councils. What do they hear from retailers? Along with quick delivery and enhanced POP materials, prepricing is a very hot topic. Trees and shrubs are being brought in line with all of the other products in the garden center. It's a time and labor issue as much as anything else, as retailers simply don't have time to price merchandise.

For some larger nurseries, especially those that have dealt with the chains, this was a challenge they faced years ago. But it's a rare independent retailer who doesn't use bar-code-reading register systems today. Briggs, selling only to independents, is just getting into prepricing with about ten customers this year. The challenge, Fran says, is coordinating the pricing requirements of their many customers with the wide list of more than 1,000 items they sell. Even giant Monrovia, which sells 75 percent of its product to independents, is in the learning mode with prepricing.

From Shrub to Art

No segment of horticulture is immune to the new plant syndrome. Nursery growers just face a tougher time than many other growers do because their crops take years to produce rather than weeks. Still, check any company's catalog and you'll find several dozen "new" listings. Nearly every company counts this as key to its success. Iseli has built its reputation on new varieties and plant forms, and Briggs, which has its own tissue culture lab for breeding and propagation, prides itself on new varieties, such as daphne Briggs Moonlight and rhododendron Northern Starburst.

But how important is new? Despite Monrovia's focus on new varieties, Pam thinks new could be overrated. "I think the trade wants the new stuff because they're more savvy," she says. "But I think the end consumer is happy with [older varieties] if you market them right."

Topiary is a perfect example. Hardly a new plant form, part of its appeal is its old-world image. Iseli Nursery, along with Monrovia and others, has done a masterful job of making topiary accessible to all gardeners.

After consumers accepted topiary, it wasn't long before other exotic forms followed, such as the multigeneric constructs that Iseli has pioneered. These are plants created by grafting two or more species together to create a whimsical, magical tree or shrub form.

You can't grow plants like this with unskilled laborers, and growers are capitalizing on this by creating an image of craftsmanship and artistry for the nursery industry. Monrovia now calls its employees "horticultural craftsmen" in recognition of their talents. André Iseli is almost fanatical in his enthusiasm for the "artisans" who work for him. He has trademarked the slogan "Where the beauty of nature meets the artistry of man," and has sprinkled his catalog with poetry and philosophy. He calls the plant forms his company creates "the manifestations of a frustrated artist"—he attended Sorbonne University in Paris.

André's newest artist is Joe Harris. "Of all the artisans in this country, probably no one is his peer for bonsai," André says with pride. "He's an extraordinary talent."

Joe traveled to Japan at age sixteen to learn the classical art of bonsai and is renowned for his skills. Recognizing Joe's genius when they first met, André nonetheless had to wait six years for the opportunity to hire him to create Iseli's new division, Matsunami-En Bonsai. Joe's goal is to create the "Tiffany of bonsai" to give garden consumers the opportunity to own real bonsai, not the cheap imitations sold at so many outlets. Prices will reflect this—the least expensive bonsai costs about fifty-five dollars wholesale.

To help ensure consumer success, they've designed a foldout brochure that explains that bonsai aren't houseplants, gives cultural care instructions, lists reference books, and even directs consumers to local bonsai societies. "It's the first time that a major nursery has taken the initiative to do this type of program," André says. "As we were instrumental in bringing topiary plants to the forefront for consumers, hopefully we'll do the same thing for bonsai."

Growing Pains

Many of these programs are in their infancy. Briggs has only tested prepricing with about ten customers, and even giant Monrovia is struggling to compete against regional competition. While topiaries may be in the spotlight today, more emphasis is going to be on how nurseries sell, not what they sell.

"Just growing plants isn't enough anymore," Fran says. "We've got to find out what our customers want. And that's more than just a nice plant."

September/October 1998.

Rootstocks: The Core of Apple Success

Laurie Beytes

The apple is one of our most important Temperate Zone fruits and one of the oldest fruits in cultivation. But don't make the mistake of focusing entirely on the varieties of apple trees that you'll offer to your customers next spring. Instead, put your effort into providing apple varieties that are growing on the proper rootstocks. Today's rootstocks are more consumer friendly than ever, offering a smaller, easier to grow apple tree with the same size of irresistible apples we've come to expect.

Most size-controlling rootstocks used now in this country have come from Europe. The East Malling Fruit Research Station in Kent, England, has done outstanding work in this field, developing a series of rootstocks that have different degrees of dwarfing for apple trees. Dwarf apple trees are produced by grafting a desired variety (such as Granny Smith) onto a specific rootstock that has been selected on the basis of its dwarfing character. They're highly recommended for home planting, as they have several advantages over standard or seedling trees. Their reduced tree size makes it easier for consumers to prune, spray, and harvest the crop. They require less space in the garden, and they usually bear fruit earlier than their standard-sized counterparts, often just three to four years after planting. Most standard-sized apple trees require up to ten years to come into production.

Some of the most recommended rootstocks are the Malling 9 or 26 for a truly dwarf (seven to ten feet) tree or the Malling 7 for a slightly larger (ten to twelve feet) tree. Rootstock recommendations, however, vary depending upon what area of the country you live in, as do varietal recommendations.

One more tip: Don't skimp on the apple trees you carry; they may very well outlive their owners. Look for one-year-old trees that are four to six feet in height and at least ⅜ inch in diameter. They'll usually grow better than smaller grades or older trees. Give your customers the choice of varieties on rootstocks that are well suited to growing in their area. And next time, maybe they'll come back for pear trees!

For more detailed free information that's specific to your area of the country, tell your customers to contact their Cooperative Extension Service. They'll be listed under either County or State in the phone book and are an invaluable resource to assist us.

Live Focus, January/February 1998.

Viburnums: Endless Variety

Laurie Beytes

To directly quote Michael Dirr from *The Manual of Woody Landscape Plants* (the Bible of woody plants), "A garden without a viburnum is akin to life without music and art." And Dirr isn't the only horticulturist who's enthusiastic about viburnums. We spoke with George Krauth, owner of Viburnums by George, located in Estill Springs, Tennessee, and he had much to say about the virtues of viburnums.

According to George, viburnums may be evergreen or deciduous, and they range in size from two to thirty feet. They can be found all over the world in places like North Africa, the Orient, and Central America, as well as right here in North America, where we have at least sixteen native species. This is a great testament to their adaptability, as they tolerate a wide range of soil conditions and can thrive in sun or shade. Viburnums are a group of plants that have no real insect or disease problems and require very little maintenance. Many varieties are available with drop-dead gorgeous flowers, some of which are fragrant. According to George, 95 percent of viburnums have fruit (berries) that is attractive and is also great for attracting wildlife. And yet, with all these great attributes, "Viburnums are greatly underused!" says George.

About 120 species and numerous cultivars of viburnum exist, so there should be something to suit virtually everyone. As we obviously don't have room here to talk about all of them, we've selected a few varieties that George recommended and that your customers won't be able to resist.

Viburnum carlesii 'Cayuga'
This cultivar has a nicer overall plant habit than the species *carlesii,* being a compact, spreading, deciduous shrub growing to five feet. It also produces an abundance of white flowers that George says are even more fragrant. Grows in Zones 5 to 8.

Viburnum dentatum 'Synnestvedt'
Commonly known as Chicago Lustre, this is a deciduous, multi-stemmed shrub. It has an upright, rounded habit and grows ten to fifteen feet tall. Beautiful, glossy, dark-green foliage, creamy white flowers, and fabulous metallic blue berries make it an excellent choice for Zones 3 to 8.

Viburnum dilatatum 'Michael Dodge'
Bright yellow berries are the real show-stopping reason to try this new variety. And the large, white, lace-cap flowers are a nice added bonus. Good for Zones 4 to 8.

Viburnum nudum 'Winterthur'
This variety was collected and selected by Winterthur Gardens in Pennsylvania. It grows to about seven feet tall and is good for Zones 5 to 9.

Lustrous green foliage, a profusion of white flowers, beautiful dark blue berries, and terrific red fall color make it a must for new varieties to try.

Viburnum plicatum var. *tomentosum* 'Igloo'

This exciting new variety is most impressive for its extremely dense, rounded habit. And when you see that rounded, mounded shape, thick with white flowers, you can figure out why it was named Igloo. Dark green foliage and bright red berries are some other assets. This viburnum will be especially nice for small gardens in Zones 5 to 8.

Viburnum plicatum var. *tomentosum* 'Pink Beauty'

This extraordinary pink doublefile viburnum is one of a kind. However, George says it will only bloom pink for those customers living in Zone 5, as it needs cold weather to attain that color. Otherwise, it will bloom white. No matter what the color, this gorgeous viburnum will grow eight to ten feet tall and has bright red berries. Give it a try in Zones 5 to 8.

Viburnums are fantastic four-season plants, featuring spring flowers, summer berries, clean foliage that often has fall color, and a nice plant habit that can even be enjoyed throughout the winter. They're an excellent choice for a shrub border, as well as for screening. The extraordinary flower displays exhibited by many viburnums make them a natural for spring sales, with berries and fall color to carry sales through the season. When you're getting ready to order plants for this spring, look for these new viburnum varieties as well as the good old varieties because you'll be hard pressed to supply your customers with a greater group of plants than viburnums.

Live Focus, January/February 1999.

Chapter 6
Feed Me, Seymour:
Plant Care & Handling

Fertilizers: Food for Plants

Margaret K. Kelly

Fertilizers provide plants with the nutrients they need to grow. The three major nutrients are nitrogen (N), phosphorus (P), and potassium (K). The amount of each of these nutrients, N-P-K, is expressed as a percent on the fertilizer package. One common formulation for vegetable gardens is 5-10-5. If this is a fifty-pound bag of fertilizer, it would contain 5 percent or 2½ pounds of N, 10 percent or 5 pounds of P, and 5 percent or 2½ pounds of K. So what are the other forty pounds in the bag? They are inert ingredients, often a clay material used to give the nutrients something to adhere to. The bulk of the material helps with applying the proper amount.

Organic Fertilizers

A fertilizer is organic if it's naturally occurring. Inorganic fertilizers are made through chemical formulation. As far as plants are concerned, all they want is their N-P-K, and they can't tell (nor do they care) whether it's from an organic or manmade source.

One example of an organic fertilizer is manure. Manure is a good source of nitrogen, and it also adds organic matter to the soil. Gardeners want to apply composted manure to their gardens.

Retailers sell manure in bags. Actual amounts vary, but dried

commercial cow manure has been reported per ton to have 42 pounds of N, 63 pounds of P, and 61 pounds of K. Dried commercial chicken manure has been reported to contain 31 pounds of N per ton, 35 pounds of P, and 40 pounds of K. Simply comparing these two manures, you can see that a bag of cow manure provides higher nutrient levels than a bag of chicken manure. Other organic fertilizers include dried blood, which has an N-P-K value of 12-0-0, and bone meal, at 4-12-0. In general, the nitrogen in organic fertilizers is available to plants more slowly than in chemical fertilizers.

Inorganic Fertilizers

Inorganic (or chemical) fertilizers also come in different types. They range from soluble to slow release. We apply different types of fertilizers for different uses. For a hanging basket that's looking light green, we would apply a liquid application of a fertilizer that's dissolved in water. The goal here is to get some nitrogen to the plant quickly. We may apply this type of fertilizer on a regular schedule, perhaps weekly. Also available are slow-release fertilizers. These fertilizers give up their nutrients slowly because of how the granules are made. They may be made up of a clay-type product or even encapsulated in polymer pellets that dissolve slowly. This type of fertilizer is applied at longer intervals, such as once a month to a pot or only at initial potting.

How Much?

The ideal way to determine how much fertilizer a plant needs is to have your soil tested by a university Cooperative Extension Service and get a recommendation. The second option is to follow the recommendation on your fertilizer package. Most give general applications for vegetable gardens, flowerbeds, and lawns.

Sweet or Sour?

It's important to keep in mind that the soil pH has to be in the proper range for plants to take up any nutrients. Most plants require a soil pH in the range of 6.0 to 7.2. This is a measure of how acid (sour) or alkaline (sweet) the soil is. The lower the number, the more acidic the soil. To increase soil pH, apply lime; to lower pH, use sulfur and organic matter such as manure or compost. A simple soil test can determine pH. Many horticulture retailers offer this service (do you?), as do Cooperative Extension Service offices. Basic kits are also available for gardeners to purchase.

Hard Focus, March/April 1999.

There's More Than One Way to Water— Which One Is Right for You?

Margaret K. Kelly

Improper watering is the quickest way to kill plants at both the retail and consumer levels. Employees and customers alike will find more success by following a few guidelines when watering.

Plants need water for their roots, but they don't want water on the leaves. Water on the leaves can promote plant diseases, the majority of which are caused by fungi. When water is applied overhead, allow time for the plants to dry off before the sun sets.

Continuous wetness promotes plant diseases. Give plants the opportunity to dry off between morning dew and any watering. Watering in the morning is considered best. Midday isn't a good time because the sun evaporates much of the water.

Long, deep soaks are the preferred method of watering. This promotes the best root development. Short regular waterings, such as ten minutes every day, encourage shallow fibrous roots and actually make plants more susceptible to drought.

There are many ways to irrigate plants, from sprinklers to watering wands to drip irrigation. Any or all of the following types will work for you and your customers, depending on need.

Oscillating sprinklers

The sprinkler goes from left to right, distributing water in a fan shape in one direction then the other. These types of sprinklers do a pretty good job of watering evenly and deeply. They provide good coverage and tend to be fairly quiet. Most sprinklers allow you to adjust the spray pattern.

Impact sprinklers

This type of sprinkler head moves under pressure in a circle, spraying water that radiates out from the center. These are often relatively noisy, but they have the advantage of being able to deliver water over fairly large distances.

Rotary sprinklers

These sprinklers are able to deliver water at very low pressure (as low as 1 psi). Water comes out in a gentle spray that's better for fragile flowers or seedbeds.

Soaker hoses

These are porous hoses that let water seep out all along their lengths. They're placed adjacent to plants, and water goes right down to the roots. This is the first type of drip irrigation most gardeners are introduced to.

Drip irrigation

Drip irrigation is definitely on the rise. The combination of community water restrictions and flexible plastics has brought this method of watering to the home garden. Drip irrigation makes the most efficient use of water. These systems consist of tubes and nozzles (often called emitters) that deliver water drop by drop. Tubes are placed along rows of vegetables or flowers, and these systems are left set up out of sight in gardens and turned on as needed.

Every horticulture retailer should offer one type of drip irrigation system. These provide the water solution gardeners seek: an efficient way to deliver water to where plants need it most. Drip irrigation systems are available to be sold as kits requiring assembly or with emitters already installed at even spacing.

Hand-held hose attachments

A virtual arsenal of breaker and wand attachments is available to choose from. Breakers vary from the basic round or fan nozzles, both of which put out a fairly gentle stream of water, to the more elaborate "gun" nozzles that can be adjusted to deliver several different types of water intensity.

Extension wands are useful for high and hard-to-reach places and can be found with either a basic on-off switch or a gun-type handle. Mist nozzles are also available for the hose end and offer varying degrees of spray fineness.

Hard Focus, November/December 1998.

Reducing Nursery Stock Replacements

Are you replacing as many woody plants as you sell? Even if you're replacing half or less, you can reduce the loss with a few precautions, says Elton M. Smith in the *Ohio Florists' Association Bulletin.*

Guarantees

If you guarantee woody plants for a certain time period, log returns by plant type so you can learn which plants are returned most frequently. In the future, you can avoid purchasing these poor performers.

When to plant

An important caution for your customers: Container-grown plants and balled and burlapped stock can be planted anytime. However, bare-root stock should only be planted when the plant is dormant, in early spring or in the fall after leaf drop.

The hole

Tell your customers to make the planting hole no deeper than the depth of the container. Its width should be four to five times the width of the soil ball, root system, or container.

Soil

Topsoil alone usually isn't sufficient for optimum root growth. Your customers should add some form of organic matter, such as sphagnum peat moss, compost, or pine bark soil conditioner, at one-third to one-half of the volume of soil replaced in the hole.

Staking

Not every new tree needs to be staked. In fact, unnecessary staking can weaken or injure the trunk. Most trees up to 1½ inches diameter will stand on their own. Trees up to two inches in diameter can be supported with two-by-two-inch stakes driven into the soil about one foot from the trunk. Trees more than four inches in diameter may need to be staked until the roots grow into the soil. Recommend three guy wires per tree tied to stakes driven into the ground perpendicular to the angle of the guy wire and attached to the trunk near the lowest branches. Don't leave the wire attached for more than two years.

Winter injury

Recommend that your customers water thoroughly before the soil freezes in the fall, especially if summer was dry. Also tell them to fertilize in October or November, then again in spring to facilitate recovery. Plants can be wrapped, sprayed, mulched, or tied to prevent various injuries.

Off the Shelf, March/April 1998.

Dispelling Vase Life Myths

Consumers and floral professionals alike subscribe to many myths and remedies to extend cut flower vase life. Remedies range from adding aspirin, lemonade, alcoholic drinks, household bleach, and coins to vase water to smashing flower stems, plunging flowers into cold or hot water, and stabbing stems with a pin. Instead of extending vase life, all of these "remedies" either harm flowers, causing them to wilt faster, or extend vase life for only a short time, says the Flowers & Plants Association, London, England.

Aspirin

Flowers take up slightly acidic water (pH of 3.5 to 4.5) more readily than alkaline water, and aspirin acidifies water. However, killing bacteria in vase water and feeding flowers is more important to extending vase life than acidifying water.

Water temperature

Water temperature extremes (plunging in hot, then cold water) stress flowers and increase the chance of faster deterioration. And water temperature determines water uptake. Lukewarm water is preferred, as it has less oxygen than cold water and travels up stems more easily.

Lemonade

Adding lemonade to vase water adds an essential nutrient for flowers—sugar. Unfortunately, sugar also feeds bacteria, which clogs stems and forms a physical barrier to water uptake, causing flowers to wilt and die. To feed flowers sugar, some people give their flowers alcoholic drinks or even champagne, which also feed bacteria.

Bleach

A drop of bleach added to vase water kills bacteria, improving vase life. But it's important to use the correct quantity of bleach, as it can actually kill flowers when too much is used.

Coins

Many people put copper coins in the bottom of their flower vases because of the myth that copper benefits flowers. Copper from the coins has no visible effect on flower longevity.

Smashing flower stems

Smashing the stem destroys the stem's cell structure, rendering the stem unable to take up water. Bacteria also feed easily on smashed stems. Smashing stems stresses flowers, causing them to deteriorate rapidly. The proper procedure is to cut stems at an angle so the flower's drinking area is increased. Flowers can drink more effectively if you slice through the cell structure rather than crush it.

Pins

Pins are used to straighten tulips and other flowers with curved stems. This produces a wound that bacteria can easily attack. Straighten tulip stems by wrapping them tightly in paper and placing them in a bucket of water with a light directly above them. Tulips naturally bend toward light and will straighten as they take up water.

What really works

To extend flower vase life, the Flowers & Plants Association recommends:

1. Cutting at least one inch off of all stems, making a slanted cut with a sharp knife.
2. Make sure vases and containers are very clean and use fresh, luke-warm water.

3. Strip all leaves below the water level to avoid polluting the vase water.

4. Always use a proprietary flower food that feeds the flowers, encourages buds to open, and prevents bacteria from growing in the stems.

5. Avoid direct sunlight, heat, and drafts.

6. Keep flowers away from ripening fruit and remove flowers as they fade.

7. Top off water and add more flower food as necessary.

Off the Shelf, September/October 1998.

Chapter 7
Retail Management

What Makes a Garden Center Great?

There's no such thing as the perfect garden center, right? There are plenty of good garden centers, but what makes a garden center great? Rather than ask industry "experts" for their opinions, we conducted a random poll of the people whose opinions may matter the most: enthusiastic gardeners who regularly frequent a wide range of garden centers and who've visited enough different ones, both great and not so great, to know what they like and what inspires them to buy. Here are some of their answers:

- "Selection."
- "A good variety of plant material."
- "Healthy, native plants; wide, well-laid-out aisles; a good water garden display; and plants laid out in a logical way."
- "Good signs and tags—nothing irks me more than not knowing what something is or how much it costs."

- "Huge selection, and plants displayed in a natural setting—not just in pots and packs."
- "Quality plant material. No matter what else you do, if you've got quality plants, the rest doesn't matter."
- "Excellent selection of not just your everyday stuff, and displays and a setup that make it easy to shop."
- "Variety. A place that carries just four hostas doesn't interest me."
- "Service, and knowledgeable staff."
- "Quality plants. If they don't have good product, I'm out of there."

A random poll, yes, but one that clearly shows that the most enthusiastic and knowledgeable garden center shoppers look for variety first—in fact, one true enthusiast said it doesn't matter if she has to wade through mud to get to the plants, as long as there's a wide variety. But those plants had better be high quality, or you'll just as quickly lose your dedicated shoppers. And having wide, easy-to-shop aisles, excellent signage, and a knowledgeable, helpful staff will help make your good garden center great.

Consumer Buzz, July/August 1998.

Keeping Ahead of the Hyper-Competition

Peter Konjoian

"Hyper-Competition in Retailing: Leadership Lessons"—Anyone in retail can relate to this title of last fall's Center for Retailing Studies Annual Conference, hosted by Texas A&M in Dallas, Texas. Our current economic cycle can't be described simply as competitive. That description falls short of what you and I are feeling in the trenches of our businesses. Instead, hyper-competitive is a more accurate expression of what we feel. Here are some highlights from the two-day conference, where leaders from several of America's best retail companies offered their ideas on dealing with today's hyper-competitive retail environment.

How Neiman-Marcus Does It

At ninety-one years of age, Stanley Marcus, chairman emeritus of the Neiman-Marcus Company, had most of the eight hundred attendees on the edges of our seats. His common sense, intellect, and communication skills were extremely impressive.

Stanley began by stating that, although the world has become dominated by technology and the technical sense, the best sense in business remains common sense. He focused on the importance of change and the ability of a successful retailer to accept and even embrace change. As owner of a retail garden center, I can relate to this statement as I find reasons why not to change our container sizes, retail layout, pricing strategy, business hours, and other strategies.

Don't be fooled by all this acceptance stuff, however, because Stanley's next point was that you had better be *decisive* when handling changes, problems, and opportunities. As he put it, "Don't nibble at problems—make a decision and don't look back." Be optimistic, he explained, because employees want to follow an optimistic leader. Be generous in your praise and encouragement. Lastly, confidence allows leaders to recognize and admit their mistakes. Don't worry about having to be perfect.

How Saturn Does It

Donald Huddler, president of General Motors' subsidiary Saturn, presented a perspective on retailing that mirrors what floriculture is currently experiencing. Just as small, independent growers and garden centers are searching for niches where they can compete in the marketplace, so, too, is Saturn trying to forge a niche by creating the impression of being a small-time, friendly car retailer.

Saturn is General Motors' attempt to brand automobiles. Think of the Saturn commercials you see on television. One shows a young lady coming to pick up her very first new car. The salesman leads her out of the showroom to a sparkling Saturn surrounded by several employees who applaud as she is handed her first set of keys. Another commercial shows a band of motorcyclists stopping at a desert diner only to find it overrun with elderly Saturn owners. The motorcyclists move on. A third shows an empowered employee halting the production line because something wasn't right.

Donald explained that only 50 percent of Saturn's marketing mix is product, price, promotion, and place. These are the four "P's" in McCarthy's traditional model of marketing, a model I learned about twenty-five years ago in a college marketing class. The other 50 percent of Saturn's effort is directed at what's called the "hot button": the sum of the shopping and ownership experiences. This button is the one Saturn is pushing in its attempt to brand automobiles. Guess what? It's working! Saturn has achieved the highest dealer satisfaction in the country for the last four years. The company also has the highest sales per facility. Employees have bought into the concept that the brand and the company are one and the same.

The auto industry is heading toward true sticker prices and no price haggling, Donald predicts. It's about time, right? Who among us wouldn't welcome this as a trend? Saturn has also learned that 62 percent of its customers are female while only 35 percent of its sales force is female. Sounds like what we are finally recognizing in our industry.

Lastly, he made a point that hit home with me because it is exactly what I've been feeling for several years: You need to have a world-class product. This is automatic, taken for granted, assumed in today's marketplace. But it's no longer a guarantee for success. Marketing your quality is now just as critical. Customers told Saturn that they wanted value over low prices. Satisfied Saturn owners have become a part of the marketing effort. They show up in showrooms, commercials, and at auto shows helping to sell enthusiasm for the Saturn brand. Something's working. Saturn has the highest customer loyalty of all U.S. automakers.

By the way, when someone asked why Saturn plays down its General Motors affiliation, Donald said that they didn't want to bring any excess baggage with them. Making reference to GM in Saturn's advertising might make consumers think "same-old, same-old" instead of "brand new."

What can floriculture learn from the Saturn story? Breeders, growers, and marketers are beginning to brand floral products. Proven Winners is doing very well with this concept. How about the shopping and ownership experience? How many of us understand that our retail outlets need to be destinations for our customers?

My mother continues to inform me that the convenience factor the grocery store offers is powerful. She inevitably bumps into one or two of our spring customers in the checkout line, and they sometimes have a plant in their cart. She tells me they usually are embarrassed to see her with their purchases, but hey, as long as they shop at our greenhouse in the spring, she doesn't care what's in their cart. Why should people drive out of their way to go to a small retail greenhouse when they can pick up a decent poinsettia or Easter lily where they buy milk and bread?

How a Small Bookstore Does It

Joyce Meskis is owner of the Tattered Cover Bookstore in Denver, Colorado, a successful independent bookseller in a marketplace dominated by national chains. Joyce spoke about leadership based on trust and how serving the community can create a niche that chains can't compete with. At the Tattered Cover, meeting or exceeding customer expectations is a religion. If you're looking for an unusual book, they'll stop at nothing to find it for you.

When the time came to move the Tattered Cover to a bigger building after serving the Denver area for years, loyal customers helped pack, carry, and unpack thousands of books to show their appreciation. Joyce has received awards for her work on First Amendment rights; the chief justice of the U.S. Supreme Court presented her with her most recent award.

How the Malls Do It

Barbara Ashley, senior vice president of retail sales for the Taubman Company, spoke about the competitive advantage of stores and malls. Taubman owns some of this country's most profitable shopping malls. In the last decade, the amount of retail shopping space in the U.S. rose from ten to eighteen square feet per consumer. Experts agree that this figure is too high; there's too much retail space for today's retail needs.

Barbara says the next phase in retailing will be consolidation. In the last ten years, mall after mall has been built in every region of the country. The "sameness" of our malls has resulted in less excitement in our shopping experience. Barbara's advice? Specialty stores should get ready to seize the opportunity!

Last year, the founder of Barnes & Noble Booksellers spoke at this conference and explained that most Barnes & Noble stores are not found in primary malls, but in small strip malls. In addition, each store is unique in its architecture, designed to fit into the neighborhood. There is no sameness to the outward appearance of the stores.

Another prediction Barbara makes is that large retailers will sell the commodity items, while the specialty retailers will sell fashion. Sound familiar? Isn't the mass market selling poinsettias and Easter lilies, while the smaller garden centers are focusing on unusual crops? This is just another version of the 80-20 rule. The mass market will sell 20 percent of product offerings that comprise 80 percent of the revenue. That leaves the remaining 80 percent of products that make up the remaining 20 percent of the revenue for specialty retailers to sell. That's a lot of products and a lot of opportunity for specialization. Barbara emphasized that a resurgence in our sense of community, our desire to return to simpler times, will drive these retailing trends in the years to come.

Women—and Men—as Consumers

The last several years have seen our industry acknowledge the importance of women in all aspects of our businesses. Understanding that women make up the majority of flower and plant consumers has shifted our traditionally male-dominated industry closer to center. It's still hard for me to think in terms of pink instead of red, but I'm learning.

Barbara Ashley offered an intriguing bit of retail trivia: The most popular classical music tape sold last year was the background music heard in Victoria's Secret stores! And, of course, it can be purchased right in the stores. That's slick marketing. If the women reading this article try and take credit for this marketing miracle, forget it. You're not the ones buying the tape. It's us, the guys. Victoria knows how men think.

September/October 1997.

Do You Have Green Profit in Mind When You Buy?

Joli A. Shaw

Are you and your competitors buying from the same plant suppliers? Have you been buying from those same suppliers for many years? If so, consider the fact you may be in a rut.

When you buy from the same suppliers season after season, year after year, are you seeing what's hot, what's new in plant material? And I'm not just talking about new variety ideas; I also mean new container ideas. Are you getting new ideas on how to use plants to differentiate yourself from your competitors? Or are you only seeing the old standards: four-inch geraniums, ten-inch hanging baskets, and those color bowls with one spike in the middle. Sure, you all have to stock the big five—petunias, impatiens, marigolds, geraniums, and begonias—but why should you offer the same white plastic ten-inch hanging baskets your next-door neighbor does? Why not ask for moss- or coco-lined wire baskets? How about selling wicker window boxes planted with trailing petunias instead of the fake terra-cotta boxes with red geraniums your competitor pushes?

You know niche products drive an industry, so why should you settle for less when it comes to plants? The standards are the base for any successful business, but make them your only offering and you've painted yourself into the same picture as your competitor—the classic Where's Waldo? game. Your customer can buy her red geranium planter box at the supermarket when she buys milk and eggs just as easily as she can buy it when she picks up towels at the discounter, nails at the hardware, or fertilizer at the nursery.

Does Consolidation Fuel Monotony?

Whether you're aware of it or not, the horticulture industry is consolidating. Growers like Color Spot, Pleasant Hill, California, which is now at more than seven hundred acres, are striving to be one-stop shops for retailers, offering bedding plants, pot plants, groundcovers, and even Christmas trees in a bid for retailers' exclusive business.

Is this the best option for you? Only time will tell, but consider this: If you have one supplier for plant material, do you have only one avenue to find out what's new in floriculture? Only if you let it be that way.

You have to be a savvy marketer and researcher. Watch consumer magazines that tell you sunflowers are back in and daisies' popularity is on the rise. Listen when people like Martha Stewart and Home and Garden Television hosts tell your consumers deep blues are the big color for home accents this season.

Bottom line: If you aren't getting new, innovative products into your greenhouse and into your customers' homes, you're lining your competitors' pockets with green from your lost gardening sales. Consumers are ready to spend. Don't send their open pocketbooks to another store simply because you're comfortable with your supplier.

Are you in a rut?

In My Opinion, July/August 1997.

How Five Top Garden Centers Beat the Mass Market

Chris Beytes

While there are plenty of good independent retail garden centers in the country, some stand out above the rest. When associations conduct tours, these centers are the highlighted stops. Their owners and managers are in big demand on the speaking circuit. And in any discussion about innovative retailing, their names are sure to come up.

What does it take to compete with the mass market and win? We asked five top retailers—Rogers Gardens in California, Lafayette Florist and

Greenhouses in Colorado, Longfellow's Greenhouses in Maine, Bachman's Inc. in Minnesota, and Molbak's in Washington state—to describe what it is about their operations that puts them out front.

Rogers Gardens: Showmanship

Lew Whitney, president of Rogers Gardens, had just returned from checking on his latest project: the installation of five life-size topiary reindeer at the busy front street corner of his Newport Beach, California, garden center.

"This is what makes Rogers Gardens different from anybody around," Lew says of the display, "our showmanship and our display gardens."

Throughout its twenty-year history, Rogers Gardens has done such a superb job of showmanship it's been dubbed "the Disneyland of garden centers." But attaining that level of quality didn't happen by accident. "From the very beginning, our philosophy has been that we want to show customers what potential lies in their garden," Lew says. "We try to romanticize gardening and show customers what they can do."

To achieve that end, the seven-acre retail site was developed into a rolling, curving series of gardens and planting areas. A large gazebo purchased from Disneyland is the focal point of a mature garden of lush plantings and water features. Retail and storage buildings are scattered randomly, and paths link everything together. No matter where you are on the property, you never feel far from a garden.

A big part of Rogers Gardens' showmanship is just that—showing customers how the plants will grow and what they can do with them. Rather than display bedding plants only in flats, one garden features thirty intersecting triangles (about ten feet on a side) on a slight slope, each planted with a different annual. Plantings are rotated throughout the year to highlight seasonal crops. Each triangle requires five flats of jumbo packs to fill.

If it's not planted in the ground for customers to see, it's probably planted in a large (fifteen gallon) decorative container, grown on to mature specimen size and surrounded by smaller plants for sale. For instance, pansies are displayed in various sizes and shapes of pots and bowls in solid and mixed colors so customers can see mature blooming plants and get ideas for using them. Plenty of packs and four-inch pots are nearby for sale.

Showmanship also comes through in Rogers Gardens' line of hanging baskets and color bowls. These aren't your typical baskets—you won't find a single plastic basket hanging anywhere. Instead, they use moss-lined wire baskets from ten to thirty-six inches. And they don't just dabble in color—

they have a thousand baskets and a thousand color bowls available for sale at any given time.

The production department plants baskets and bowls working from prototype designs created by Lew or his staff. Each design is carefully planned by color, cultural requirement and growth habit to make a long-lasting, attractive container. They only plant twenty or so of each design to keep them fairly exclusive. They also do one-of-a-kind containers.

Seminars are another part of Rogers Gardens' "show." "We want people to be successful gardeners, and we're willing to show them how," Lew says. Weekend seminars and demonstrations draw up to 150 attendees starved for good information. Weekday demonstrations may be more specific or discuss seasonal topics. Often a seminar on a crop will lead to a cooking demonstration.

Lew says he works hard to not only stay up with current trends but also to set trends. For instance, they've built a strong interest in lettuce, not only for kitchen use but also as an ornamental. "Product differentiation is the essence of [our] game," Lew says. "If Home Depot carries it, we're no longer ahead of the game."

Lafayette Florist and Greenhouses: Back to Basics

"It's a people industry, not a flower industry," Brian Wheat says of running a retail garden center. People, specifically the people who work for his family's company, Lafayette Florist and Greenhouses, Lafayette, Colorado, are key to the company's success. The business, started by his wife's grandparents in 1949, serves Denver- and Boulder-area consumers.

Good information and good employees to dispense it are major factors in Lafayette's success, Brian says. His employees are instructed in a "back to basics" approach to customer service. At the minimum he expects "please" and "thank you" from every employee. He also preaches an approach to customers that puts the emphasis on making them feel comfortable and trusting.

For instance, he says, when a customer is looking at a flat of petunias, an employee shouldn't ask, "You need some help?" Instead, she should show some interest with, "Boy, isn't that a great series!" The customer will feel the employee knows and likes plants and is there to help her.

Another aspect of exceptional customer service is being able to "read" customers—giving them just the level of commitment and attention they want you to give them. "It's key to train your employees to figure out each customer's individual needs," says Brian. Rather than treat each customer as an individual, most retailers operate at extremes, either pestering customers or ignoring them. At Lafayette, "We fawn all over them if they want us to, and if they don't, we back off and let them do what they want," he says.

An employee handbook spells out details of the company, the job, and how employees are expected to treat customers and each other. Lafayette has built up a reputation in the area as a good place to work, with friendly people and a good, clean work environment, so Brian rarely has to advertise job openings. He's also not afraid to let potential employees know they probably won't get rich in this industry.

But for those dedicated employees who are in it for more than money, payoff can come. Brian pays bonuses when business is good. Employees are kept informed of financial goals and expansion plans and how well business is doing to meet those goals. They also see that Brian and his family are putting profits back into the business, not into their own pockets. Being involved in financial decisions helps build employee loyalty, as does the business's forty-seven years in the same small town (pop. 18,000).

"[The employees] really care about the business," Brian says in praise. "They don't see it as a brick and mortar business; they see it as their historic hometown business they have to protect from all the retail giants."

Meeting customers' needs also means meeting their schedules. Lafayette is open seven days—8:30 A.M. to 7 P.M. weekdays, Saturday until 6:00 P.M. and Sunday until 5:00 P.M. Brian says you can't complain about beating the competition if you aren't keeping pace with them. "Too many people close their doors early and then complain that they don't have enough business."

Meeting that schedule can be tougher on the owner than on the employees. But Brian says retail is a tough business. "If you go home at night and say to yourself, 'Thank God I don't have to think about my business until tomorrow morning,' maybe you shouldn't be in business."

Longfellow's Greenhouses: Maine's Largest

In a state where winter is longer than the growing season, a greenhouse is a nice place to visit. And when that greenhouse is the largest in the state and is overflowing with homegrown product, it's even more attractive.

Scott Longfellow, Longfellow's Greenhouses, Manchester, Maine, says his brand new 14,000–square foot retail greenhouse, combined with his 80,000 square feet of production greenhouse space, is one of Longfellow's biggest assets. "The public is drawn to us for the shopping experience. It's a great feeling after winter for customers to walk through our greenhouses."

Now in its nineteenth season, Maine's largest retail grower is in the competent hands of the second generation, Scott, and his wife, Sandi, who planned the popular retail area. But if it hadn't been for a trip to Molbak's in Washington, the calling card retail greenhouse might have been a traditional—and typical—New England barn.

Scott explains: "Three years ago I was in the process of trying to decide what we would use [for retail space]. I walked into their place and said 'Wow, this is it. I'm in love with it.'" He also took a tour of British garden centers for more inspiration and to see the idea in practice.

They scrapped the barn plans and put up a 98-by-144-foot three-bay Nexus/National greenhouse for both plants and dry goods. White Exolite panels cut 60 to 70 percent of heat and light to make for a more comfortable shopping environment. Clear panels are used over the plant areas, and Polygal covers the sides. A heat retention/shade curtain keeps the house cool during the day and warm at night. Scott reports their first season with the new facility was a great success.

Customers aren't limited to just the retail greenhouse, they have full access to all of the production area (free-standing X. S. Smith houses) and can pull plants from anywhere, sometimes even from carts about to be shipped to wholesale customers. Scott doesn't mind one bit.

"The freshness and opportunity for choice is a real big plus to my customers," he says. "It's like buying apples. If you pick an apple off the tree, it's going to taste better to you than the one from the fruit stand or the grocery store." Customer access also forces Scott and his staff to keep production areas clean and neat.

Like nearly all retail growers, Longfellow's prides itself on a big selection—"You won't find a better selection in the state," Scott says—and high quality. Big selection is important in a state where the spring season is a matter of weeks, not months. If gardeners don't have their planting done by June 1, they feel they're too late. Buying direct from the grower also reassures customers that they're getting top quality, Scott says. And the flexibility lets him better serve their needs.

While the rest of the country has battled the big chains for a decade, Scott just got his first taste of mass-market warfare when Wal-Mart moved in five miles away in the spring 1994. He reports that dry good sales were hurt slightly—they haven't dropped, but they haven't increased as much as other categories. Bedding plants' sales haven't been impacted, and perennial sales are up 32 percent.

Retailing in a state that lags behind much of the rest of the country does have its advantages. Scott says he's able to watch how other independent retailers have been impacted by the mass market and adjust his strategies accordingly.

"There's no chain that's going to take care of its customers as well as I take care of mine."

Bachman's: A Destination

While other retailers want to be as unlike the mass market as possible, Todd Bachman is capitalizing on what the chains have done right. Like The Home Depot and Circuit City—retailers that pride themselves on being one-stop shops—Todd is focused on making Bachman's a complete if-we-don't-have-it-you-don't-need-it retail destination. Today his family's 110-year-old business operates twenty-three floral stores of various sizes and descriptions throughout the Minneapolis area, all designed to meet the needs of today's consumers.

Today, being a destination is important for any retailer, Todd explains. Shopping patterns and habits have changed; people have hectic, busy schedules, and convenience is very important to them.

"The type of customer who's shopping us is a destination customer," Todd continues. "They're interested in a horticultural 'superstore' where they can find all of their gardening, landscaping, floral, and gift needs in one location."

Bachman's answer to consumer convenience fits that description perfectly—a minimum five-acre site featuring floral, garden center, and landscape products all at one location. They currently have six such outlets strategically located in high-traffic areas throughout the Minneapolis/St. Paul area, a short drive from the majority of the Twin Cities' population. The "superstores" feature a 30,000–square foot retail area for floral, gift, and garden center hard goods. Another 50,000 square feet of outdoor space is for garden plants and nursery stock.

But having twenty-three stores isn't what makes Bachman's a horticultural destination. Todd explains that it requires incorporating many products and services into one location, all centered on enhancing the home environment. That means carrying almost every product gardeners could want and giving them ideas for using those products through creative displays and educational seminars. "We're not just a store that only sells fresh flowers or arrangements or garden products. We try to position ourselves to enhance [the customer's] living environment," he says.

While Bachman's has invested heavily in the superstore concept, they also know there are other ways to take advantage of consumers' need for convenience. To that end, they operate full-service floral shops (1,000 to 1,500 square feet) in leased space at eleven grocery stores and also have seven branch floral/gift stores located in regional malls and strip centers. More stores are planned, including two in new, high-end Chicago-area grocery stores.

Knowing what customers want to buy is as important as knowing where and why they buy. Like other retailers, Todd pays attention to trends that influence his customers and finds ways to capitalize on them. One way is to advertise specific varieties by name, such as Impulse impatiens.

"Our customers are smart," says Todd. "They're reading not only the horticulture magazines but also the interior design magazines that talk about annuals and perennials by name. We like to use the names, too, so there's an association there by the customer." He adds that when customers have success with a particular plant or series, they will look for it again. And specific variety names differentiate Bachman's from other retailers who are only advertising impatiens.

Multiple stores offer opportunities, Todd says. He can reach more consumers, and he can standardize growing and purchasing and get volume prices on purchases. But whether you have one store or one hundred doesn't matter to customers, Todd stresses. What does matter is this: Are they excited about coming in the store? Does it pique their interest in your products? Can they find what they want? Can they get the information they need? Are employees nice to them?

"All of those factors set you apart," Todd concludes. "Just because you've got six or twenty or thirty locations doesn't make that much difference as long as at each location you're doing the job right."

Molbak's: Ambiance

When his greenhouse is filled with contented customers sipping cappuccino and enjoying the classical music, Egon Molbak knows he's accomplished what he and his wife, Laina, set out to do thirty-nine years ago—create the most pleasing, relaxing, garden atmosphere possible at their Woodinville, Washington, retail garden center.

Like Bachman's, Molbak's is a destination. But Egon has taken a different road to that goal, focusing on ambiance. Get that right, he says, and combine it with top-notch quality and employees, and sales will take care of themselves.

What is ambiance? Egon defines it as the feeling and personality of a store. In Molbak's case, it means feeling less like a garden center and more like a garden. "People come here not necessarily with the intention to buy," Egon says, "but because it's a place to visit." Molbak's ambiance is so appealing, they're listed with Seattle-area visitor's bureaus as a tourist destination.

Molbak's ambiance comes in large part from their 104,000–square foot retail greenhouse area. Meticulously arranged and kept spotless by diligent employees, customers can hardly pull a plant from a bench before the hole is filled back in. Light classical music plays throughout. Practically any plant variety customers could want is on display, grown nearby at Molbak's own 200,000–square foot production greenhouse (400 varieties of garden plants, 900 varieties of foliage at last count). Outside, customers can browse 100,000 square feet of nursery space.

But Egon says Molbak's doesn't push sales. Many customers stop by only to enjoy a cup of espresso or cappuccino and a sweet from the full-service coffee bar. They can then relax in the conservatory area surrounded by lush tropical foliage and the soothing sound of waterfalls, birds, and Strauss waltzes.

"We like to see people relaxing and having a good time," says Egon. "That creates a good feeling between us and the customer."

More ambiance comes from the 3,500–square foot gift area. Molbak's has always had a reputation for carrying the largest and finest selection of garden products, gifts, and home décor items in the Seattle area. Where the typical home improvement center carries about 40,000 different products, Molbak's new inventory tracking software lists 65,000 SKUs, not including plant material. Egon says when they first moved from wholesale to retail in the early 1970s, "We decided that, whatever we did, we weren't going to dabble in it. We were going to be into it with both feet."

Molbak's latest product line adds to the ambiance. Concrete sculpture, always a big seller, has led them into "real" stone sculpture, original pieces carved by world-renowned artists and displayed in a gallery or garden setting, depending on the piece.

Like many other retailers, Molbak's is big into events. Along with their Fairy Tale festival, held for three weeks in October, and the Poinsettia Festival, which features 10,000 poinsettias in twenty-seven varieties, is the July Two-for-One sale, a major event for Molbak's. Egon says it's not done to clean out the greenhouse, but it's a promotion they actually grow product for. Four hundred customers wait for the doors to open at 9 A.M. sharp— "It's a stampede," Egon says. Many have stopped by earlier in the week to plan their shopping strategies. The sale is a moneymaker, probably their biggest volume day of the year.

Molbak's is known as the inspiration for many other retailers in the country. Where does Egon go for inspiration? "You pick up something wherever you go," Egon says of his world travels. Molbak's also has an outside board of directors made up of merchandising professionals from other industries that provides guidance and inspiration.

Egon and Laina Molbak themselves are a key ingredient of Molbak's ambiance. Their Danish background, personal tastes, and sense of style have made Molbak's the retail landmark it is today. Egon says that, while they've often been imitated, Molbak's will never be duplicated.

"Who you are, hopefully, comes across in what you do."

Seattle Retailers Contend with
New Competitors and Established Leaders

Joli A. Shaw

Working from a small core group of enthusiastic, hard-core plant-buying customers, retailers in the eastern Seattle suburbs of Woodinville and Bothell have traditionally benefited from an idyllic, Britain-like climate and discerning, dedicated customer base. This season was no exception, after a somewhat questionable spring.

Perhaps unbelievable to some, in spring 1997, Seattle was hit with record rainfall. But despite its misnomer as the "rain capital of the country," Seattle's typical annual rainfall is actually less than that of New York City. And coupled with record cold temperatures, that extra moisture brought retailers one of the worst springs on record.

Despite all this, consumers apparently were in the mood to spend, and they did so as this year's bedding plant sales season extended on through July and into August. The eleven retailers in the area we visited were enjoying steady traffic from consumers searching for the perfect plant.

Gardeners in Woodinville and Bothell (combined population 35,999, according to the 1990 census) aren't your typical consumers. Many are savvy, knowledgeable customers who shop for plants year-round and have high expectations of not only plant quality but also selection and availability.

Consumers in this area are well educated—Microsoft, Boeing, and a slew of medical companies are housed nearby. These multibillion-dollar employers enable their employees to boast sizable spending potential: The median household income in Woodinville is $57,403; in Bothell it's $37,159. Compare to Seattle's median household income of $29,353. And while home building has waned a bit, consumers are gearing up to decorate their landscapes after completing their interiors during the housing boom of recent years.

Enter the Big Boxes

Hungering after this burgeoning market, big-box stores like The Home Depot and Eagle Hardware and Garden have broken into the Seattle-area market in the past two to three years. With them came the battle for the lowest plant prices in town. Armed with substantial promotional budgets and an eye for green profit, these mass marketers quickly caught on with impulse buyers and new gardeners through prolific ads and flyers.

When we visited, hanging basket prices were more than ten dollars lower than what local independents were charging consumers. Competition between chains was fierce, with frequent ads quoting competitors' prices to declare themselves the low-price leader. And the potential for more sales is certainly there with some product maintenance and employee training.

The Market Leader

Retailers in the Seattle area have something to contend with that is unlike most other markets in the U.S.: Molbak's, one of the country's leading and most innovative independent garden centers, makes its home right in Woodinville. The selection, display creativity, and customer service are legendary, making it a formidable opponent even for retailers who would dominate in any other market. Molbak's is also listed as a tourist destination in the Seattle-area Chamber of Commerce guidebook!

The store is divided into many departments that often carry the same product lines seen in full-line independents, but with a floral flavor—cushions, artwork, gift items, etc. all center around flowers. Each department has its own storefront, register, and entrance from outside of the building—a garden center strip mall. Displays take advantage of major consumer trends: One display incorporated pots, dishware and clothing with watermelon themes, another used myriad shades of consumers' current favorite hue: blue. Consumers often remark, "I was there for hours; I could have been there for days."

Trends

Two undeniable trends pop up as you shop garden centers in Woodinville and Bothell: wooden containers and fuchsias. Northwesterners love their lumber, and it shows in garden center selection. Nearly every garden center we visited—chain or independent—offered wooden containers of some sort at every price point. One independent offered cedar hanging baskets available in fifty different types of plant material for $29.99. Mass marketers tended to offer the more typical impatiens or petunias, but at a $17.99 price designed to make them the low-price leader.

Fuchsia is the other product no Seattle-area garden center is without. Several independents even offer so many varieties that their selection is alphabetized—their customers know their fuchsias! Fuchsias are offered in every form—from two-inch starter plants to ten-inch hanging cedar baskets to even a fuchsia tree.

Bottom line in Seattle: This market has yet to truly develop in terms of competitiveness. The still-new big boxers have yet to significantly impact independents' dominance. The increased competition that will probably evolve as the big boxers set roots in the marketplace stands to broaden consumers' choices at every outlet.

September/October 1997.

Raleigh Independents Stand Strong

Debbie Hamrick

In Raleigh, North Carolina, lackluster sales in March due to a cold, wet, late spring were compensated for by mostly sunny weekends in April and May, giving lawn-and-garden retailers an excellent spring season. Known as the City of Oaks, this graceful southern town has grown up over the past two decades into a chic metropolitan area known for its Old South charm. Modern infrastructure and an influx of some of the country's best and brightest talent have made the area a Mecca for start-up technology firms. Unemployment is less than 2 percent.

Year-Round Opportunities

The exact origin of Raleigh's dynamic horticultural scene is difficult to pinpoint. Perhaps it's due to the influence of North Carolina State University's Department of Horticulture; perhaps it's also because gardening is nearly a year-round activity. For retailers, Raleigh's season begins in the fall with pansies and garden mums. Because of an active commercial landscaping trade in which office parks seem to compete with one another using pansies and other seasonal exterior color, each day consumers on their drive to work pass hundreds of commercial landscapes dotted with bright yellow and blue masses. The not-so-subliminal message is to plant pansies so their homes will be as beautiful as their offices. Fall is also the main selling season for lawn care products and seed (fescue and fescue/bluegrass blends being the main varieties).

The Raleigh gardening season continues into the winter months when camellias and winter-flowering vines make their appearance and slowly progresses through the late winter and early spring with a procession of color that peaks when dogwood and azalea blooms are at their height in mid-April. Annuals then become the mainstay—especially impatiens and fibrous begonias, two reliable annuals that provide masses of color in the oppressive heat and humidity. For summer, four-inch and six-inch annuals take over.

Understanding the procession of the seasons in this mild southeastern climate isn't easy for buyers in offices. Perhaps that's why several mass marketers were still displaying pansies and perennials (*Phlox subulata,* for example) geared for March sales at the end of April, when displays should have been stocked full of hanging baskets, color bowls, bedding plant flats, and spring- and summer-flowering perennials.

Profiling the Retailers

Raleigh independent garden centers are as dynamic as the gardening season. From the expansive, arboretum-like setting of Homewood Nursery to the metropolitan location in the abandoned Amtrak station of Logan Trading Company or the display gardens, modern architecture, and wide expanses of Rake & Hoe Garden Center, northern and central Raleigh gardeners have a diverse set of retailers from which to chose.

Most independents' store interiors are dedicated to upscale giftware, garden ware, bird feeders, and containers in a range of price points. While most stores also offer a selection of bulk goods such as fertilizers, stepping stones, pine straw, and pine bark, it's the DIYs and Kmart that have most aggressively pursued these commodity items. As a matter of fact, it's difficult to miss the half dozen or so semitrailers that litter the parking lots beside The Home Depot and Lowe's garden centers.

Perusing five independent garden centers, three mass marketers, two DIYs, and one supermarket yielded interesting market trends on the last Saturday in April. Many outlets were short on Boston ferns, the single most popular hanging basket and a plant that graces the front porches of thousands of eastern North

Annuals that tolerate Raleigh's oppressive heat and humidity are the mainstays of the spring market in this southeastern city.

Carolina homes. Proven Winners material in any container size—four-inch pots, combination pots, or baskets—was also in short supply. Wave petunias, another hot spring item in 1998, were in good supply at several independents but generally sold out elsewhere, as were Fiesta double-flowering impatiens, another great seller. With the exception of a few combination pots consisting of annuals at Wal-Mart, the only selection of combination pots featuring higher end vegetative material such as verbenas, *Bacopa,* or vegetative petunias was at Homewood Nursery. On this weekend before Mother's Day, most independents were showing a good selection of hanging baskets and bedding plant flats.

Comparing Prices

	Average price/plant	10 in. basket	10 in. basket
	cell packs	Low end	High end
Independent garden center	$0.301	$12.18	$13.57
Home center/DIY	0.205	6.32	7.30
Mass marketer	0.252	5.75	7.75
Supermarket	0.331	8.99	9.99

Population Explosion

Even though Raleigh is an upscale market and growing in excess of 10 percent every two years in population base, independents took a market share hit when The Home Depot and Lowe's came to town. Since 1990, Raleigh's population has increased 44,000, and the lawn-and-garden retailing scene saw the addition of three large-scale garden centers: Atlantic Avenue (independent), The Home Depot, and Lowe's.

While central and north Raleigh may be overstored in lawn and garden currently, several factors point toward long-term market growth. Among them: The median age of the population is 31.9 years (prime home ownership years); median family income is in excess of $50,000 per year, and more than half of the working population earns more than $35,000 annually. Also on the plus side for long-term growth is the fact that the area's retail sales are increasing at a rate of 10-plus percent per year, and nearly 70 percent of the population base is employed in white collar or government jobs. Large employers in the area include IBM, Northern Telecom, Glaxo-Wellcome,

American Airlines, SAS Institute, Bell Northern Research, U.S. EPA, and Alcatel Network Systems.

Population growth is projected to increase another 33,000 people by the year 2000 and 76,500 people by 2010. Major highway infrastructure projects are set to create new traffic and retailing patterns, which could offer existing independents opportunities for expansion as well as opportunities for competitors to enter the market.

In the short term, Raleigh's population is rapidly catching up to the retail space expansion in lawn and garden of the last five to seven years. In the future, independents will be set to do battle with mass marketers in the struggle for the dollars of central and north Raleigh's affluent gardening community.

July/August 1998.

Success Secrets from England's Retailer of the Year

Mike Cooling

As the winner of England's 1997 Retail Nursery of the Year Award, I'm delighted to be able to share some ideas that are behind Cooling's Nurseries' success.

Our background begins with a typical small family business in the suburban village of Chislehurst, some nine miles from London, where we grew tomatoes, mums, and bedding plants, all of which were sold from the one-acre site.

In the early 1960s we introduced self-service sales of bedding plants, and from this beginning we opened a garden center in 1961 with an initial stock of tools, fertilizers, and other hard goods that cost fifty-five cents, a figure that horrified my father, who thought such expenditure would rapidly lead to bankruptcy. However, business expanded, and within a few years we had to purchase another nursery to produce plants for sale in our expanding garden center.

By the mid-1980s, our garden center was in need of either rebuilding or relocation. In view of the rapidly increasing value of the land for building, we decided to sell and move eight miles to our present fourteen-acre site, which we were able to purchase from a well-respected firm that had specialized in trees, shrubs, and conifers for over forty years. Although a new garden shop had been recently built, there was little on the site but two small bungalows and several old greenhouses. One bungalow was used as an office and gift shop, the other as a thirty-five-seat coffee shop.

This design enabled us to plan a new layout based around car parking at the front of the site, leading to a greenhouse-style shop (for checkouts and dry goods), with plant sales in the area behind the shop. The production area was consolidated at the rear of the sales area with access by a new concrete road to allow free flow of growing materials to the production greenhouses and outside container shrub beds.

The idea of a circular route was continued from the glasshouse area back to the sales area, thus allowing the movement of finished plants directly into the sales area by the way of five-tiered trolleys that we then unloaded directly onto the sales beds or benches.

Specialized Selection

Although we're called a garden center, we have a very definite policy of selling only those items necessary to cultivate good gardens. These include peat, potting composts, garden equipment, stakes, and trellises. This is contrary to most United Kingdom garden centers, which heavily stock garden furniture, gifts, barbecues, and seasonal Christmas items.

Our policy is to grow very good plants in a wide range of varieties and species, and our sales efforts are based around that production. Again, this is contrary to the general trend in garden centers, which are becoming more and more retailers rather than horticulturists. This has generally led to a very limited range of shrubs, trees, and plants, with only the very common and well-known varieties being offered.

By going against this trend, we're attracting very keen gardeners who are more and more knowledgeable and who require the latest and best varieties as soon as they're available.

To provide this range of varieties, we constantly visit nurseries and gardens throughout Europe to obtain new ideas that we can promote, and by having our own in-house production, we ensure that we promote and then are able to meet the demand. Nothing is worse than stimulating demand and then not having the stock to meet that demand.

Subtle Marketing

Our marketing and promotion is a major feature of our business; it's particularly remarkable because it's not noticeable! It's based on our consumers talking to their friends; we don't buy any newspaper advertising. We aim to make the shopping experience a very enjoyable one. We do this as follows:

1. We provide easy parking: a high-quality surface for 140 cars plus unlimited grass for peak seasons when we often have over 400 cars.
2. We have clear signage and a simple site layout, good paved paths throughout, enabling customers to find what they want easily with friendly staff visible to give guidance and advice.
3. The paths are kept very clean. (We use a garden vacuum cleaner.)
4. Arthur's Coffee Shop is named after my father, who founded the company. This is now housed in a new building built in 1997 on traditional oak beam construction using more than thirty-four tons of green oak for roof timbers. This magnificent building, which cost $443,016 to build, has seating for one hundred inside, with the possibility of at least an equal number on lawns and patios outside in good weather. Food is served "cafeteria style" (self-service), although orders for hot items are prepared and brought to the table. We try to make most of our cakes in the kitchen, which promotes the "Old English teashop" atmosphere. There's no music, but there is an attractive outlook onto the gardens. Included in Arthur's are the rest-rooms, which are of high-quality finish and meticulously maintained.

5. The site is totally without steps and is accessible to wheelchairs; we have a fleet of five wheelchairs, including a self-propelled one, available for free customer use.

6. We offer lectures on many aspects of gardening that are given by myself, my son, or famous gardening personalities. Most of the talks are free and are repeated once or twice for each subject as we work to capacity audiences of 110 for most occasions. Thus, the Saturday talk at 11 A.M. is repeated at 2 P.M. on Wednesday, and if it's a popular subject, an extra session is offered on Wednesday morning. For celebrity speakers, we sell tickets to cover the speaker's fee, usually five dollars per ticket.

7. Any retail company stands or falls by its staff, and we take great care to ensure that our people are polite and attentive, dressed in clean, neat uniforms, and will either give sound advice or immediately find a member of the team to advise a customer. Our staff also helps select plants and load heavy goods into cars. Heads of departments are, with one exception, diploma holders from horticultural colleges. Other permanent staff members are trained by working four or five weeks each year at a horticultural college over a period of two years.

8. Plant quality is vital to the "wow factor" for customers who need to be able to see the quality and size immediately. This quality is backed by clean, fresh, informative labeling, with eight-by-six-inch bed signs that we make ourselves using computer graphic prints, and plastic labels are attached to each plant. They're easily created and printed in-house using a computer and thermal printer.

Keeping Customers Interested

"How do you keep the customer enthusiasm going?" is a question we're frequently asked. The answer is to build a "part of the family" feeling. We do this with our newsletters, which are produced three or four times a year and are four to eight pages in length. The first page is always a letter from me that has my signature at the end. In this, we list our latest developments: where we've been, staff promotions, and training successes. Also included is family news, such as the birth of the first of the fourth generation in our business.

The most important part of a mailing list is to encourage people to give their names and addresses, and this we do by producing lists of dates for forthcoming lectures and demonstrations in the newsletters. Therefore, when people want to know when we're giving these talks, we tell them that we'll happily send them lists if they give us their names and addresses.

As an extension to our regular lecture program, we also invite any organization to bring a party of not less than thirty-five members along, and we'll arrange a special talk for them, but only when the garden center is open. This brings in new customers, and if nothing else, they use the coffee shop before or after the event.

Since we opened the new site in 1990, our turnover has increased by an average of 15 percent annually up until 1997, and our 1997/98 sales have risen to a 30 percent increase, despite many prices (bedding in particular) being almost static for three years, to a total of $3.5 million, excluding tax.

Our plans for the future are based around improving and extending the display gardens around Arthur's Coffee Shop so that we can give a wider range of practical demonstrations using established planting areas. Our aim is to ensure that our friends (customers) continue to talk about us, which will, in turn, continue our growth.

March/April 1999.

Give Me New and Fresh, or Give Me Calyx and Corolla

Joli A. Shaw

At this year's Super Floral Show in Columbus, Ohio, top retail critic Peter Glen offered a painfully accurate look at our industry's visual presentation, customer service, and product knowledge. He spent January to June visiting and analyzing mass-market retail floral departments throughout North America and came up with some insightful criticisms and suggestions for improvement. One of his main messages: For all the time we spend preaching about fresh products, we allow the vast portion of our industry to grow stale—our marketing, our employees, our product selection. We, and our customers, are bored with them. "Refresh yourself!" says Peter. If you're not constantly changing and constantly keeping your people and your customers excited, you're dead.

We Have a Lot to Learn

In marketing campaigns alone, the floriculture industry is pitifully far behind the rest of the world.

"New York is the most refreshed city in the world," says Peter. The marketing ideas you see there are some of the most off-the-wall, forward thinking, and profitable in the world. A billboard in Times Square now costs $2.4 million. The fronts of taxicabs are being sold as advertisements. Why aren't flower and plant retailers as smart as Old Navy, which bought every coffee cup in New York? And Calvin Klein bought every popcorn box in New York theaters. All of these potential advertising venues, and we're still doing circulars!

Putting products in the "wrong" place is a stroke of genius, says Peter. Those ads above urinals and on the insides of bathroom stall doors? Hey, we have to read something.

The same is true in retail stores. Put a rack of flowers or plants in the meat department. By putting something in a place we wouldn't normally expect to see it, you make customers see it afresh.

"Garden ads are the soberest ads in the world," says Peter. You have to make people smile and laugh to get them interested in your product. Why shouldn't we create ads like the Mercedes Benz ad that consists of a close-up on a smiling rubber duck in water, with the tagline, "For $62,500, you can have fun."

You not only have to refresh your marketing and sales, you have to refresh your employees. Peter used the Macy's Flower Show in New York City as an example: The store imported tropical flowers, brought in Hawaiians to hula in the aisles, and put leis on customers. "The first people to get excited were the employees," says Peter. Because they were excited, the customers were excited, and they bought more product.

Refresh Yourself

How can you refresh yourself and your stores? Peter offered several guidelines:

- You are responsible for your own freshness.
- Be more curious.
- Place yourself in the wrong situation more often, so you can come back and refresh your situation.
- You are in the art of making yourself visible.

Here's something to think about: Five years ago, the average American spent 142 hours each year just browsing in stores, Peter says. Last year, customers spent only 40 hours. That's a quarter of the time! What are you doing to make sure those hours are spent in your store?

In My Opinion, September/October 1998.

Old Flowers: Know When to Dump Them

J Saxtan

Dumpage is a part of doing business with fresh products such as baked goods and produce, and discounting the price of products that have minor damage or are less than perfect can reduce some losses. But with floral products, the only thing to do when they've been around too long is to dump them. Trying to salvage a few cents on the dollar for dying or damaged flowers or plants isn't worth the overall damage it can do to your floral department's image.

Consumers are realistic when it comes to floral purchases—they don't expect them to last forever, but they do expect them to last for five to seven days. Any longer than that, and they're impressed with the quality of your flowers; any less than that, and they question the value not only of the flowers that didn't last, but also the lasting value of any future purchases of flowers. "Why bother?" they'll say. "They'll just die in a day or two, and I'll have to throw them out."

Unless you're getting your flowers delivered directly to the store from the grower on the day that they're harvested, your "fresh" flowers may be up to a week old by the time they're placed on sale in the store. For example, flowers shipped from the West Coast by truck can take five to eight days from harvesting before reaching the retail level in the Midwest. Even when shipped by air, the time lapse can be three to six days.

This isn't to say that your fresh flowers aren't fresh or that you should find new suppliers—they've probably got at least another week of storage life left in them and a consumer vase life of another week, especially if proper care and handling procedures are followed. This is simply to say that you can't expect too much from cut flowers. Some will last longer than a week in storage or on display; some will last less. Just remember that once a flower or bouquet is sold to a customer, that customer expects it to last up to another week.

Generally speaking, you can expect properly stored and treated flowers to last seven to ten days in your store and still be salable enough to offer customer satisfaction once they are in the home. Some flowers, especially some exotics such as *Anthurium,* may last longer than that, but others won't last a week. Many factors influence a flower's longevity, including good care and handling practices before receiving product at the store or central processing area, storage and care once it's at the retail level, treatment with preservatives before and at the retail level, and the degree of maturity when the flower was received. If you're unfamiliar with a certain flower or if you want to know more about the storage life of flowers you're selling, ask your supplier.

Check for Freshness

Dating floral products for internal information can help keep products fresh and indicate when a product is ready to be put on sale or dumped. A product that has been stored for five or more days probably shouldn't be displayed for more than another five to seven days.

Dating alone won't assure that all of the flowers on display are fresh enough for sale. Visual checks must be made periodically, and wilting or dying flowers and greens must be removed from the display and dumped. If one flower in a bouquet is dying, remove it immediately or it will speed up the demise of the rest of the bouquet. Check for broken necks, wilting petals and leaves, browning of petal edges, and general poor appearance.

Products that have been on display for five or more days and still look fresh should be considered good candidates for a special—they'll probably remain fresh-looking for a few more days and then start downhill. There's still enough time for them to provide customer satisfaction in the home, but if you wait too long to move them, they may end up only being good enough for the garbage heap.

Take Your Cue from Wholesalers

If you ever have the opportunity to visit a floral wholesaler late in the day, walk outside and inspect his trash. You'll find lots of flowers being dumped—flowers that many produce managers would think they could still sell. But a floral wholesaler's business and reputation are based on the quality (translated as freshness) of the products he sells. When he's had the flowers too long and knows that they won't last as long as they should at the retail level, he dumps. And he doesn't like to throw away product any more than you do.

One problem several wholesalers who service supermarkets have mentioned is that the produce department just hates to face up to the necessity to dump flowers. "They just won't do it," they say. "They can't seem to plan flower dumpage the way they plan it for other produce." Perhaps it's the beauty of flowers that causes hesitation, or maybe it's the fact that no one is going to eat flowers, so they aren't going to be harmed by those that are "spoiled." But the harm comes in selling flowers that aren't going to live up to customers' expectations.

Certainly floral dumpage can be reduced by inventory planning, by receiving shipments several times a week instead of all at once, and by implementing proper care and handling procedures. But there are always going to be bouquets that have stems with broken heads (sometimes damaged by customers poking through them) and surplus stock that just doesn't sell. You may buy a hundred mixed bouquets and only sell ninety-five of them in a reasonable amount of time. What do you do with the other five that are now less than fresh? If each entire bouquet still looks fresh, you could put them on special. If some flowers are OK and others aren't, you could take the bunches apart and reassemble three or four decent bouquets, then put them on special. You could make up some corsages with the decent blooms and hope to sell them soon. Or you could do what you should do: dump them. The labor involved in trying to salvage a few flowers probably isn't worth the effort.

You wouldn't sell spoiled meat, broken light bulbs, or rock-hard bakery goods, not even at bargain-basement prices. Aside from other considerations, you just wouldn't want the image of selling less-than-usable merchandise. The same holds true for floral products. Don't sell them when they're already over the hill. If they look less than fresh, they're already past any point of salvation. Dump them. Selling floral goods that are damaged can only damage your store's reputation.

March/April 1998.

Chapter 8
For the Birds

Inviting the Birds Home

Margaret K. Kelly

Lifelong birder Chris Brothers of Falmouth, Massachusetts, filled us in on how your customers can attract birds to their yards. Here's her list of essential tools and how to use them.

Birdfeeders

A birdfeeder is the absolute minimum for attracting birds. If customers are going to have only one feeder, they should select a tube feeder. This consists of a tube with various openings and perches where birds can dine. A tube feeder will attract most backyard birds such as cardinals, chickadees, blue jays, and house finches. Look for a feeder made out of Lexan, a tough plastic that squirrels can't chew through. The challenge of bird feeding is attracting birds while discouraging squirrels.

A flat-shelf feeder is desirable for attracting cardinals and mourning doves. Unfortunately it's almost impossible to keep squirrels off of this feeder.

A dome feeder looks like a bowl with a baffle over the top. If the baffle is low enough, the birds can get in but the squirrels can't.

A hopper feeder, generally made of cedar and resembling a little house, is the most squirrel-proof. It has a lever that automatically closes the feeder if a heavy bird or squirrel stands on it.

Thistle feeders have small holes to hold the tiny thistle seed. They may either be stand-alone feeders or bags called a thistle socks, which can be hung from another feeder. These attract goldfinches and siskins.

The best suet feeders are made from wire mesh with plastic coating. You can buy either premade suet blocks designed to fit in a feeder, or you can get suet from a butcher. Suet will attract woodpeckers, chickadees, blue jays, and, yes, squirrels.

Where to Hang?

The best place to hang a feeder is suspended from a string hung from two points in the yard (like a clothesline). Another option is to hang a feeder from a metal post in the ground.

The worst place to put a feeder is on a wooden post, as squirrels and cats can easily climb these. Don't hang a feeder from a house for the same reason. Feeders should be near trees and shrubs so birds can survey the feeder before approaching, but not so close that squirrels and cats can jump onto the feeder.

What Seed Should You Feed?

The one seed that attracts most birds is sunflower. You can select either black oil sunflower, which has the advantage of having a high fat content, or striped sunflower, which costs less.

Cracked corn will bring in mourning doves. If quail and pheasant are in your area, sprinkle cracked corn on the ground to attract them. The corn will also lure squirrels.

Chris suggests that you buy seed in bulk and make your own mix. Many budget birdseed mixes have a high percentage of milo seed, which birds push aside. Check mixes for how much desirable seed they have—don't shop just by price per pound.

To attract the best assortment of birds, use a tube feeder filled with sunflower seed, a thistle feeder, and a suet feeder, and sprinkle cracked corn on the ground.

Birdbaths

Birds need a source of water, especially during drought or in dry areas. A birdbath can be placed right on the ground, which allows other animals to drink from it, or hung by a chain or placed on a pedestal. Birdbaths need to be heated or brought inside in the winter, or they'll crack. Bubblers are available for birdbaths since birds are attracted to dripping water. A birdbath should be cleaned every few days.

Additional items for the backyard birder: hummingbird and oriole feeders, birdhouses (make sure they can be easily cleaned out), metal storage cans and scoops for seed, brushes for cleaning feeders and birdbaths, binoculars, bird guides, and lots of landscape plants.

Hard Focus, July/August 1998.

Birding Hobby Isn't Chicken Feed

Does the birding section of your store consist of a few plastic feeders and some stale sunflower seeds? If so, you're missing out on what Ray David of Birdwatch America says is the nation's second most popular pastime, right behind gardening: backyard bird feeding. Here is a bird's-eye view of birding from Ray:

- Sixty-three million Americans feed wild birds.
- The number of wild bird specialty retailers has doubled in the past three years. This market segment got its start because traditional retailers weren't doing the job.
- The birding products market is estimated to be about $20 billion per year.
- More than 40,000 retail outlets in America sell birdseed.
- The most expensive birdseed is Niger, retailing at one dollar per pound, and Americans buy more than sixty million pounds of it every year.
- Upper latitudes—New England, the Midwest, and the Pacific Northwest—are the strongest birding areas of the country.
- Two strong trends in birding specialty shops are garden art and water gardening.

Consumer Buzz, July/August 1998.

Serving Your Birding Customers

"Bird-feeding consumers are upgrading, giving birds better product," says Sonny Pennington, president, Pennington Seed, Madison, Georgia. Where ten years ago feed was made with ingredients designed to keep prices down for consumers, today's bird feed has twice to three times as much in the bag, and the ingredients are the highest quality. Redbird mix, thistle, and other specialized products are gaining popularity.

In response, companies such as Pennington are upgrading their packaging, offering reusable bags that are easier to handle. Products are packaged in standup bags that can be properly merchandised on the shelf. Pennington has gone to pouches, which Sonny says have more perceived value. Their mixes are in colorful bags with a cutout window so consumers can see the seed inside.

So, what bird feed should you stock for your customers? Here's Pennington's guide to birds in North America and what they feed on. Why not make up a chart to display in the garden center?

Bird	Zone	Feed
Baltimore oriole	Central and eastern U.S. from Canada to mid-southern U.S.	Natural springs nectar
Blue jay	East of the Rockies from Canada to Gulf States	Wheat/milo, sunflower seed
Cardinal	Eastern U.S. from Canada to Gulf States	Sunflower seed
Chickadee	Eastern U.S.	Sunflower seed, suet
Common flicker	Canada to southern U.S.	Suet
Downy woodpecker	Alaska and Canada to southern U.S.	Suet
Evening grosbeak	Canada to southern U.S.	Sunflower seed
Fox sparrow	Alaska, Canada to central U.S.	Wheat/milo, millet
Goldfinch	Southern Canada to southern U.S.	Sunflower seed, thistle
Hairy woodpecker	Alaska, Canada to southern U.S.	Suet
House finch	Canadian border to mid-southern U.S.	Sunflower seed, thistle
House wren	Southern Canada to southern U.S.	Suet
Ruby-throated hummingbird	Southern Canada to Gulf States	Natural springs nectar

Off the Shelf, January/February 1999.

Bird Is the Word

Jennifer Derryberry

More than the flutter of wings or the tweet of the beak, it's the ring of the register that makes birding worth your retail while.

Offering basic birding fare—simple feeders and seed—could boost your bottom line a bit, but sticking to your plant expertise may make more sense, not to mention dollars. Establishing a display of plants and nursery stock that attract the nationally visible hummingbird, for example, capitalizes on our knowledge.

"Consumers need the right birdfeeder, feed, flowers, and plants to get interesting birds into their yards," says George Petrides, manager of the Wheaton, Illinois, Wild Bird Center. The specialty birding store is part of the Glen Echo, Maryland-based franchise, which has more than one hundred stores in about twenty-five states. "For lawns without trees, consumers need shrubs and flowers, in particular," George says.

By partnering with a bird store, you can promote complementary product lines—your plants and their specialty feed—to give customers maximum value and service via coupons, seminars, and advice. You also gain access to a powerful demographic: Nationwide, the Wild Bird Center reaches more than 525,000 consumers with its newsletter.

Off the Shelf, July/August 1999.

Wildlife-Attracting Plants That Fly off the Shelf

Joli A. Shaw

What should your customers consider when trying to attract butterflies and hummingbirds? Butterflies are attracted to scent, and certain plants give off smells that tell butterflies they may be able to find nectar in them. Hummingbirds respond to visual stimulation and particularly like the color red. Conveniently, many red flowers are good sources of nectar. Here are some suggested plants from Monrovia Nursery, Asuza, California and Heritage Perennials, Abbotsford, British Columbia. (Starred varieties attract both butterflies and hummingbirds.)

Perennials: *Caryopteris incana, Teucrium fruticans* Azureum, *Asclepias tuberosa, Salvia grahamii, Echinacea purpurea, Lavandula dentata candicans, Perovskia atriplici-folia, Buddleja davidii** Pink Delight or Black Knight, *Salvia greggii* Furman's Red, *Achillea millefolium* Paprika, *Achillea* hybrid Moonshine, *Gaillardia* x *grandiflora* Goblin, *Coreopsis verticillata* Zagreb, *Rosmarinus officinalis* Huntington Carpet, *Agastache, Alcea,* allium, *Anaphalis,* aquilegia, aster, *Chelone, Echinops, Eupatorium, Hesperis, Heuchera, Kniphofia, Liatris, Lobelia cardinalis, Malva,* monarda*, *Physostegia,* rudbeckia, *Scabiosa,* sedum, and solidago.

Rudbeckia and echinacea will keep your customers' gardens abuzz with activity.

Annuals: ageratum, *Cleome,* cosmos, fuchsia, heliotrope, *Mimulus,* nicotiana*, petunia, salvia (red), and verbena.

If your customer is looking for shrubs or vines, try these: *Campsis, Lonicera,* or weigela. All attract hummingbirds.

Both companies have publications available to help you sell more plants for butterfly and hummingbird gardens. Heritage's list is made up into an attractive brochure. Monrovia Nursery has a new poster and flyer listing plants and even suggests a layout for the garden.

Off the Shelf, March/April 1998.

Birdbath & Beyond

Jennifer Derryberry

Hummingbirds are to birding what daylilies are to the floral and garden business: You'll find them nationwide. Hummingbird concentration decreases as you cross the country from the West, explains George Petrides, manager of the Wild Bird Center, Wheaton, Illinois. In New Mexico, for instance, you'll find about twenty species; east of the Mississippi River, the ruby-throated hummingbird is the lone hummingbird.

The Pennsylvania State University College of Agricultural Sciences reports that an array of flowers attract hummingbirds mid to late summer. Spotted touch-me-not, trumpet vine, cardinal-flower, garden phlox, coralberry, hollyhock, Turk's cap lily, rose of Sharon, butterfly milkweed, butterfly bush, bee-balm, and impatiens draw the hummingbird into the suburban area, says Margaret Brittingham, associate professor of wildlife resources.

The right feeder is also important to attracting birds. The signature red plastic feeder with a nectar of one part sugar and four parts water keeps the hummingbirds coming back. A birdbath with a mist attachment also entices hummingbirds. What to watch: Beware cats and pesticides.

Supply and demand are at work in birding, as well. According to *Birding Business* newsletter, the right birdseed is critical to attracting birds, and presumably, their watchers. Here's a list of fine birding fare:

- Black oil sunflower
- Niger
- Gray-striped sunflower
- Safflower
- Shelled sunflower
- Peanuts
- Milo
- Cracked corn
- Millet
- Mealworms

Off the Shelf, July/August 1999.

Chapter 9
On Golden Ponds

Selling More Water Gardens

Joli A. Shaw

Water gardening is set to explode, says Greg Wittstock, president/CEO, Aquascape Designs, West Chicago, Illinois. But for retailers to take advantage of this potential boom, they'll have to change their merchandising and sales strategies for water gardens.

"Right now, retailers are spending too much time with their customers [selling water gardens]. The industry average is one and a half hours spent with each customer to get them up and running with a water garden," he says.

Why is that a problem? Because most of that time is spent educating customers about water gardens. "The time you spend with the customer should be time you spend upselling them to larger products, not telling them how to care for fish in the winter," Greg says.

There are so many choices in water garden types and sizes that consumers need assistance to buy water gardens: what size pump goes with what size filter to go with what size pond, etc. The key, says Greg, is to provide take-home literature and videos so consumers can be educated outside of your store and selling area. Giving customers materials that answer common questions and describe the best sizes and setups for water gardens saves time. They'll have time to review the options at home in their own time without feeling pressured, and when they come back to your store, they'll be ready to buy.

Water gardens aren't a spontaneous choice. Most often, you don't have to make a sale on the first visit. Give them literature with your logo, phone, and address on it to encourage them to come back to you. "Educate them outside of the store," he says. "Instead of spending an hour and a half making a $200 sale, spend that time making a $1,200 sale to a consumer who knows what he wants."

Most water garden consumers want to get their feet wet and start out small. The pro of this is that consumers keep coming back to buy bigger items. Take advantage of these return customers by cross-merchandising. "These consumers usually leave with impulse purchases such as geraniums or garden accessories," says Greg. "When you create a water feature, you create a need for future landscaping."

Consumers don't need just water gardens. They need aquatic plants to put in the pond and terrestrial plants for around the edge of the pond. Many people also later put in a deck or patio around the feature. And often this means adding trees, shrubs, or bedding plants to make the feature more visually appealing.

Another reason retailers have difficulty retailing water gardens: lack of manufacturer support. "If you just get a new stand to display the products, you're telling customers they have to assemble the product themselves piece by piece without any assistance," says Greg. "In today's time-crunched world, you can't force customers to do that." That's why he and many manufacturers are producing complete kits that provide everything consumers need, including step-by-step videos, to create their dream water gardens. With the kits, all consumers do is choose a size and location in the yard, and everything else is taken care of.

Off the Shelf, January/February 1998.

Demonstration Ponds Inspire Ideas All Year

Sherri Bruhn

It's interactive gardening at its highest level, a miniature ecosystem of plant and animal life. Consider the ascetically pleasing sounds of a small-scale waterfall and croaking frogs. Water gardening is on the rise, and there's nothing like a display pond to help fuel the trend.

Jeff Rugg, former owner of water garden retailer Nature's Corner and now zoologist and horticulturist with Pond Supplies of America, Yorkville, Illinois, says display ponds are great ways of giving people ideas of what to look for. He adds that water gardening is appealing to a variety of consumers. There's a wide spectrum of interest coming from apartment dwellers with whisky barrel ponds to homeowners with small koi ponds or quarter-acre ponds.

"It's a summertime fireplace," says Jeff of a water garden. "It's not just sitting there and watching the grass grow."

Jeff suggests building a display that looks like a pond someone would have in his or her own yard. He stresses the importance of having the proper growing conditions for the plants. Keeping the correct light and temperature

in an indoor setting is key to an eye-catching display. One common mistake to avoid is having too much water in the tub. Jeff says this makes the display harder to maintain and can damage plants. He recommends a water lily display that's two feet deep in a four-by-eight-foot tub, with water only two or three inches over the top of the pot, allowing the leaves to grow over the rim. Shoreline plants can be displayed in shallow trays with only a few inches of water around the bottom of the pots. Also, don't grow plants too close together. Crowding cuts off sunlight and causes leaves to rot.

Demonstration ponds are year-round displays that should be in a visible area where customers can hear the waterfall and where they'll be tempted to feed the fish. Benches and patio furniture can add to the ambiance as well. What kind of plants should you use? Jeff recommends lotus for good visual impact even when not in bloom, a selection of hardy and tropical lilies, vertical plants such as cattails, and annuals such as canna lilies for their colorful leaves and flowers.

Off the Shelf, March/April 1999.

In Water Gardening, Knowledge Sells

Gary Wittstock

A flowing waterfall, a floating water lily, a peaceful reflection of surrounding life—it's no wonder water gardening is booming. If you're serious about selling water feature components and supplies successfully, it pays to learn your subject.

Ask your suppliers for videos and handouts that you and your employees can learn from and then offer to your customers. Some suppliers even offer consultations to retailers, on-site instruction, or hands-on training for installation.

Expertise sells because older pond building methods are still around. "People are still putting in plastic pools with stone around the edges and a pump in the middle. There are no fish; the plants don't grow, and the water is green," says Jeff Rugg, Nature's Corners, Naperville, Illinois.

The newer "ecosystem method" is a complete system that produces a more lifelike pond setting. Displaying a completed pond that's clean, natural looking, and shows the parts working is a key way to display and attract interest in the products you sell. "If you can display a thriving pond indoors in a store, imagine how much easier it would be outdoors," Jeff says.

To make it easy to get all of the needed components without having to spend a great deal of time figuring out plumbing sizes, etc., many companies also offer kits that include every element of a complete pond: skimmer; filter; waterfalls and pump; underlayment and liner; rocks and gravel; and seed bacteria. Provide your customers with complete lists or packages of the requirements they need for a successful pond.

Gear your displays to the new pond builder by pushing top-selling plants and fish, or suggest upgrades such as lights or fountains to current pond owners.

Photos of finished water features are another excellent tool. On a bulletin board in the store, Jeff displays photos from customers showing ponds built using the products he sells.

Off the Shelf, September/October 1997.

Water Gardening Essentials: What Customers Should Know before They Buy

Margaret K. Kelly

Spring is coming, and so are water garden sales. How can you sell more water garden supplies? By making it easy for your customers to create a beautiful water feature in their yard. Knowing what they should consider before buying can save you headaches and returns, and will increase your sales volume. Here are some facts to know when selling water gardens.

Volume

How big is the pond? It's essential that water gardeners know the volume of their ponds. How many gallons does it hold? Every treatment, fish, and plant addition will require this piece of knowledge. The best way to determine the pond's gallonage is to use a flowmeter when initially filling the pond. The flowmeter measures the amount of water that passes through it. This can be rented or may be standard equipment for pond installers.

The next option for determining pond volume is to calculate length by width by depth. Use average depth to calculate. Unlike swimming pools, ponds aren't standard shapes. When calculating volume, divide the pond into several more uniform shapes for length and width. This might include one long rectangle and two small squares. Once you have volume in cubic feet, multiply it by 7.5 to calculate the approximate gallonage.

Depth

How deep should the pond be? This is partially determined by what your customer plans on doing with the pond. It should be a minimum of eighteen inches. Any less and it will freeze solid in the winter or become overheated in the summer. The types of plants and fish you're incorporating will determine the depth you need. Koi fish require a minimum depth of three feet and may prefer more. Remember that making the pond deeper makes it harder to see the ornamental fish in the pond.

pH

pH is a measure of acidity. It's measured on a scale of 1 to 14. Below 7 is considered acid, above 7 is alkaline, and 7 is neutral. Fish will tolerate a wide range of pH from 7.0 to 8.5. For koi, a pH of 7.2 to 7.8 is ideal. Because a pond has many living things in it—namely fish and plants—that influence pH, measuring pond pH is trickier than measuring garden soil or swimming pool pH. To determine pond pH, take a sample at sunrise and again at sunset; pH will change dramatically over the course of the day. These two readings give a more useful picture of pond acidity. Generally, pH should be checked once a month or after changing 20 percent of the water. Temperature, number of fish, number of plants, and aeration can all influence pH. It's best to take a close look at these factors and manipulate them before putting any acid or lime into ponds.

Hard Focus, January/February 1999.

Plants for Perfect Ponds

Laurie Beytes

It's easy to stock all of the hard goods you need for creating a water garden: liners, pumps, fountains, etc., but make sure you don't miss the boat when it comes to the plant material you have on hand to go in them. While water lilies may be the main attraction, other plants are also essential for a truly great display. Your customers will need to select from three types of water garden plants to have a successful, self-cleaning water garden.

Underwater Plants

Also known as submerged or oxygenating plants and sold in bunches, these plants act as natural filters for your water garden. Oxygenating plants naturally absorb the carbon dioxide that algae need to survive, so the proper proportion of them in a water garden will help keep the water clean and algae free. One bunch of underwater plants is required for every square foot of water surface area in ponds under a hundred square feet; use one bunch for every two square feet of water surface area in ponds over one hundred  square feet. Here are some of the more common underwater plants to choose from: anacharis (*Egeria densa*), cabomba (*Cabomba caroliniana*), mare's tail (*Hippuris vulgaris*), hornwort (*Ceratophyllum demersum*), and tape grass (*Vallisneria gigantea*).

Marginal Plants

Also called shallow-water or bog plants, these plants are used as plantings along the edges of the water garden. They provide necessary shade and hiding places for aquatic life and also camouflage the edges of the water garden and create a natural effect. This is a fairly large and diverse group of plants. Here are a few common choices: cattails (*Typha angustifolia*), horsetail (*Equisetum hyemale*), pickerel weed (*Pontederia cordata*), and umbrella palm (*Cyperus alternifolius*).

Water Lilies

The stars of the show and probably the No. 1 reason that people want to create their own water garden, water lilies provide shade for the water garden, which helps keep it cooler. They also provide surface coverage to help prevent oxygen loss and evaporation.

A water garden should have one water lily for each square yard of water surface area. During the summer, a water garden should be 60 to 70 percent covered with water lily foliage.

There are water lilies hardy for USDA Zones 3 to 10 that are perennial and will come back year after year. They bloom during the day with flowers that float right on the surface of the water. Flowers range in shades of white, yellow, pink, orange, and red.

Also available are tropical water lilies, which are the largest and showiest of water lilies, showing off their flowers well above the surface of the water in all colors. They'll grow in Zones 3 to 11 during the summer but are frost tender, so they can only be grown year-round in Zones 10 to 11. Some are day bloomers, and some are night bloomers, but all are extremely fragrant.

Live Focus, January/February 1998.

Lowdown on Pond Liners

Margaret K. Kelly

Liners make it possible to have a pond anywhere, regardless of soil conditions. No need to install some sort of concrete structure. Flexible (sheets of material) or preformed (molded) liners are available. Flexible liners conform to the shape of the area that's been dug out. Preformed liners are inserted into an area dug to conform to them. Once the liner is installed, there are no differences between the two types. Selection comes down to customer preference and which material they feel comfortable handling. Some consider flexible liners to be more fluid and naturalistic, but it needn't be that way. Landscaping determines the final look.

Many products will hold water—shower curtains, roofing materials, and the like—but the ability to hold water is only part of the question. The full question is, Will this product hold water and support fish and plants? The industry refers to the products as being "fish friendly." An unfriendly product is one that kills fish, generally by giving off toxins. Has the material been tested for use with fish? If it's safe for fish, it will be fine for plants.

Liners are made from plastic (which includes polyethylene—high density, low density, vinyl, polypropylene) or synthetic rubber. Some of the technology for these products comes from developing landfill liners and roofing materials. Ask suppliers about the expected life of their liner material. Is there a warranty on the material when used in a water garden?

Find out if the material breaks down when exposed to sunlight. What has been used for ultraviolet (UV) stability? Plastics break down when exposed to sunlight. How is this being addressed in the product? UV inhibitors can be added, but large percentages of additives can weaken a material.

Stocking a complete line of pond-related materials is critical to successful water gardening sales. This includes pumps, filters, pipe, decorative stone, water plants, and fish. How much of this you carry and your level of experience with these items will help make your sale. If you aren't going to carry the full line of accessories, whether individually or in kits, prepare a "shopping list" that the customer can take to a hardware store to get the needed items. Tell them which stores in your area stock the needed items.

Knowledge really does sell these higher maintenance items. Have you ever put in a water garden? Has the employee who will be answering the water gardening questions? Put a water garden in your store or at that employee's home so your employees can learn about the process. Take step-by-step pictures of the installation. Then photograph the pond in each of the four seasons.

Do you feel comfortable carrying fish? Work with a supplier who can back you up as you learn about them. Or you may have an employee who is already a fish enthusiast. The same holds true for aquatic plants. Suppliers want you to be successful with these products. Find out all you can from them.

Making sure your customers have the proper foundation for their water gardens can make the difference between $200 per sale and $1,200 per sale and keep your customers coming back for upgrades.

Hard Focus, March/April 1998.

Chapter 10
Merchandising & Display: Creating the Look That Sells

Dressing up at Retail

Chris Beytes

There's a big difference between just wrapping a plant in plain green foil and creating a truly innovative, eye-catching, value-added product. Fortunately, that difference doesn't depend on money. Classy plants and great displays can come from simple, low-cost, readily available materials.

Julie Wilkinson, Highland Supply's director of education and creative marketing, recently spent a day with *GrowerTalks* to show us colorful ideas for using common "selling tools" from Highland such as Speed Covers, Metallized Film, and Sculpting Ribbon to make uncommon plants and displays that almost beg customers to buy.

Creating an Impression

"It's not just the quality of your product, it's the quality of your presentation," Julie says. Consumers face so much choice today that you have to go all out to catch their attention.

Do your current displays work? Julie recommends you quantify them by watching how customers react to them. Do they pass by with only a casual glance, or are they stopped in their tracks? Record how long it takes to sell out most of the display. A good display can move many times the product of an average one. When you have one that works, keep it full—"You can't sell from an empty wagon."

Change displays regularly. What was eye-catching two weeks ago won't be noticed this week. Focus on holidays, seasons, special sales, or specialty items. Use displays to draw customers into strategic areas of your business.

Colors and Textures

"People are usually more motivated by color than by variety," according to Julie. In fact, since many plant purchases are made on impulse, the color of both the plant and its packaging can influence a purchase decision.

Metal

Metal continues to be popular with consumers. The chrome and glass look of the past has given way to gold, copper, pewter, brass, and silver finishes, along with anodized colors. Metal adds richness to any product while acting as a "flashlight," bringing light and sparkle into dark areas of your store. Pots, foils, Metallized Film and Sculpting Ribbon are available in metal colors. Metal is also considered to be "earthy," Julie says, tying in with the trend toward natural materials.

The "natural" look

Along with metals, natural materials with earth tones such as paper, burlap, stone, and terra cotta are very popular with consumers. They also work well to enhance the already natural image of plants, while their coarse textures contrast well with smooth metals or high-gloss colors.

Creating image

Use different colors and textures to create or even change a product's image. White daisy mums are very traditional and when decorated with a burlap Speed Cover and gingham ribbon, they have a casual, country look. Wrap the same daisy in black Metallized Film with a gold foil bow and attach some balloons, and it becomes a high-class New Year's Eve decoration. Put it in purple and teal foil with a coil of gold foil Sculpting Ribbon, and it becomes a festive party gift.

Rarely does a holiday or occasion have one accepted "feel" or color combination. The perfect Valentine's Day plant might be decorated with soft, romantic pink or hot, passionate red, depending upon a customer's age or marital status. Consider all the options when decorating for holidays.

Choosing colors

"When it comes to color, everybody wants to be different, but they're afraid to be different," says Julie. The fact that green Speed Covers are still Highland's top seller proves this.

Julie uses gold and teal Speed Covers on yellow, red and bronze flowering plants. Rather than clashing, these colors work well together because gold and teal are members of the complementary families yellow and blue. Also, rather than clashing, teal against the green foliage actually makes a very natural combination of the colors of sky and grass. The oceanic color is also very relaxing, and the unexpected combination adds interest and draws attention to the display.

If you're afraid to use color, Julie recommends buying a color wheel to help you experiment with new combinations. Start out by exploring color families—pink, lavender, purple and red, for instance.

GrowerTalks, *May 1996.*

Julie's Merchandising Tips

Chris Beytes

Julie Wilkinson, director of education and creative marketing for Highland Supply, shared some invaluable ideas to make your products even more appealing to your customers.

- High-end consumers prefer color coordination—similar color shades. Price-conscious consumers prefer lots of color variety.
- Try something besides foil: metallized, printed, and clear films offer another alternative. Use metallic elastic string (available from film suppliers) to attach to pots.
- Don't skimp with materials. A few cents more for film or ribbon can add dollars to the product's perceived value.
- Strategic placement of colors gives more impact to your displays. Don't put matching colors side by side; put complementary colors near each other to provide contrast.

- Don't be afraid to use Speed Covers. Adding a dollar's worth of enhancements will keep your plants from having that "chain store" look.
- Price fairly. Consumers will pay for added value if they perceive it as added value. But they won't let you gouge them.

GrowerTalks, *May 1996.*

Ten Profitable Guidelines for Bedding Plants

1. Check for need of water. See if plants need water as soon as they arrive. If they do, water thoroughly so that soil is completely moist. Caution: Splashing water may cause flower spotting.
2. Display in a protected area. Put plants under a structure that shields them from wind and rain. If they're displayed outside, they're subject to a complete loss at any time.
3. Place off the ground. Avoid putting plants on asphalt parking lots, as asphalt absorbs heat on sunny days, causing plants to dry out quickly. Display plants at a convenient height for customers to shop without bending down.

4. Label plants. Make sure plant type, variety, price, planting exposure, and other recommendations are clearly visible.

5. Maintain area daily. Each day, check plants for need of water, yellow leaves, and old blossoms. Remove any material you wouldn't personally buy.

6. Fertilize after seven days. If plants are on display for more than a week, use a soluble commercial fertilizer at the recommended label rate.

7. Keep top-quality stock. Consolidate merchandise frequently so it doesn't appear picked over.

8. Provide information. Use handouts, signage, POP, and other strategies to tell your customers how to grow the plants you sell—when to fertilize, how to space, and how to arrange groups according to variety and color.

9. Continue sales through summer. The season doesn't end on June 1. Tell your customers annuals can be transplanted well into August and will still look attractive before frost.

10. Keep your sales area attractive. If product looks poor, sales will be poor. Don't let dead plants stay in your display area. Nothing discourages a sale like a flat of dead or dying material.

Off the Shelf, March/April 1999.

How to Offer the Perfect Pot Plant

Kim Moreland

How can retailers offer exactly what consumers want in pot plants? What kind of packaging or merchandising method makes a product a success? We asked Justin Dautoff, Nurserymen's Exchange, Half Moon Bay, California, "How do you make consumers want to buy your pot plants?"

Justin says to have a successful product, his company has three general principles. First and foremost is: "You have to have a quality product." Customers won't buy anything—no matter how good the packaging is—if the plant is poor quality.

Next, he states, "A diverse selection and a unique product line will allow you to differentiate yourself from competitors." He says Nurserymen's Exchange stays away from bare-bones basic lines to offer premium products.

Finally, Justin says you must focus on service, no matter what you're trying to sell. Experienced salespeople, helpful clerks, and knowledge of market demands will go a long way in making a customer happy.

He reports that the most significant trend in pot plants is a strong demand for upgraded products, with a focus on greater quality in the market, as opposed to being price-driven. "Because the economy is doing well," Justin notes, "people are willing to pay for enhancements" in pot plants. You can add specialty picks, premium pot wrapping, or even items such as cookie-bouquet picks to a pot plant to increase its value and attention-getting potential. Because pot plants are being used more often today as gift items, customers are interested in a full product. Justin says, "They want the special pot, bow, and plant, not just the plant."

Off the Shelf, July/August 1998.

One Dozen Ways to Make Your Customers Impulsive

Chris Beytes

Impulse is key to expanding flower sales. Research shows that 85 percent of all floral sales are made on impulse, which means that you've got to make the most of every opportunity to put your product in front of the customer.

Here are twelve tips from a presentation at the Floral Marketing Association's 4th Annual Convention, held this summer in Houston, Texas.

1. More surface area. Micro-market your floral sales by using your entire store. Set up plant displays in areas formerly reserved only for hard goods.

2. Front end. Merchandise your store's entrance and checkout area with special, attention-grabbing displays.

3. Fresh look. Changing your displays often—not just the plants, but also the fixtures—will give the impression you've got new and exciting things for sale. Versatile fixtures let you expand and contract displays seasonally. Employees should know how and when displays are going to be set up, how long they are to be maintained, and when they are to be taken down.

Uniform signs hanging above the merchandise helps customers easily find what they're shopping for, and attractive signs in each product leave no question about identity or price.

4. Signage. Clear, eye-catching signage is essential. Keep signs consistent across all displays for a professional look.

5. Audio. Stimulate impulse sales by using your intercom or PA system to promote sale items or various departments. Speak slowly and clearly, and make the message easy to understand. Be descriptive; use words that evoke pictures and feelings.

6. Planning. Plan your sales and display strategy before you bring in product, then order aggressively and be willing to take some risks. Keep the display full, attractively signed and priced, and check it frequently for freshness. "You can't sell from an empty wagon."

7. Cross-merchandise. Set up displays using deliberate impulse strategies, such as with containers or fertilizers. Remember, many impulse sales are often driven by occasions like birthdays and parties. Merchandise accordingly.

8. Price points, demographics. Variety is important. Offer special items at a variety of price points based on your customer demographics. And never take anything for granted. Don't assume your customers will only spend so much. They might surprise you.

9. Freshness, quality. Spent flowers won't attract impulse sales, and a plant that doesn't last won't generate repeat business. Strive to carry only the freshest plants. If you have a discount area, keep it well away from the front of your store. It can send the wrong signal to customers.

10. Color-blocking. Take a cue from the grocery store produce department and organize displays in broad stripes of color rather than just by item. This gives a strong visual representation and a place for the eye to focus. Vertical striping is more pleasing to the eye than horizontal striping.

11. Fragrance. Use the natural fragrance of flowers to attract customers. Put cut roses or other scented flowers at the checkout counter. Use fragrant plants near the entrance to capture customers' attention when they first come in.

12. Name associations. Take advantage of celebrity marketing by using tags or names that represent a current movie celebrity or a popular song. Cause-driven marketing is also successful; offering a percentage of the sales of an item to a particular charity or organization is a positive way to stimulate sales.

GrowerTalks, *In Brief, October 1996.*

POP: Placement Is Key to Success

You've just accepted delivery on the latest product, which comes complete with a sophisticated point-of-purchase rack system bedecked with all manner of attention-grabbing signs, tags, and banners. Now what do you do with it? Where and how will it impact shoppers most effectively?

The Point Of Purchase Advertising Institute (POPAI) has done research into consumer buying habits and has published a booklet on maximizing in-store advertising effectiveness. Here are some of their tips.

POPAI says consumer buying habits play a critical role in where you put POP fixtures and materials. For example, their research shows that while 58 percent of grocery store customers tend to visit most or all of the store aisles when they shop, at mass merchants they tend to only shop in the aisles where they plan to look for a product. Your goal should be to lure them into more areas of your store and encourage more impulse spending.

This is where signs and fixtures come into play. Use the most frequented areas of your stores to promote products that are kept in lower traffic areas. This is the idea behind cross merchandising, which grocery stores do so well. But consider going beyond just putting one brand of rose fertilizer near your rose bushes. Use signage to lead customers to where you keep the rest of your rose fertilizers and other rose products.

As all consumers know, the front of the store, especially at checkout lines, is the traditional favorite place for POP use. This is the best place for small and single-serve items. That doesn't just mean candy. Seed packets, trial-sized containers of fertilizer, and other inexpensive products are perfect for around your registers. Some stores target the captive audience in the checkout line with video presentations. Valley View Farms, Cockeysville, Maryland, has video monitors above the checkout lines that play excerpts from television segments featuring retail greenhouse manager Carrie Engel, now a local celebrity.

One underused place for POP is the floor. Use graphics, footsteps, or other symbols to lead shoppers to areas you want them to shop. This is especially effective with children, judging from the snack food aisles in the grocery stores.

Consumer Buzz, September/October 1998.

Ten Commandments of Effective POP Signage

1. Look for romance; sell the "sizzle." Signs must catch the consumer's eye quickly, so the message must have pizzazz. For example, "I'm dreaming of a red Christmas" on a sign for red poinsettias or "From the Old World to your world" on a display of terra-cotta containers.
2. Write facts, not fiction. Rather than using advertising cliches like new and super, find out the facts and put them on your signs.
3. Explain what isn't obvious. Signs should keep customers informed about new products or benefits that aren't immediately apparent.

Petunia Purple Wave attracts attention when a sign of explanation invites customers to experiment with its spreading, cascading habit.

4. Help your customers buy the right product. If you sell functional products, use signs to help your customers know which product best meets their needs.

5. Help customers comparison shop. Good-better-best signs showing the benefits of each are a great way to help your customers make smart buying decisions.

6. Always ask, "What will it save?" By using signs to provide reasons for a purchase, you can help customers feel good about their buying decisions. Beyond the price value, will a product save time? Stress? Make it known.

7. Don't belabor the obvious. If you're displaying product in a selection of colors, don't waste your sign space telling customers it's available in assorted colors.

8. Stay positive. Your goal is to welcome people to your store. Turn negatives into positives, i.e., "No smoking" becomes "Please, no smoking. Our plants are breathing."

9. Use product packaging as a source for features and benefits. Let the vendors' marketing work for you.

10. Break all the rules if it fits your strategy. If you're aiming for the image of an old-time general store, use signs and lettering the way old-time stores did. Just be consistent.

Source: Insignia Systems, Minnetonka, Minnesota, a promotional and point-of-sale materials vendor, in Furniture Today. *Off the Shelf, November/December 1997.*

What Color Are Your Sales?

J Saxtan

Color sells, and you can use it beyond simply stocking pretty flowers and plants in your garden center. According to one expert, color accounts for 60 percent of a consumer's buying decision. This means that if you use colors strategically, the selling job is already more than half completed for you. Try these color-use tips to move your product off the shelves.

Red

Red vies with yellow for being the "fastest" color we see. It's aggressive, regal, and makes objects appear larger and nearer than comparable objects of another color. How can you use red?

Use red to call attention to things. Red signs or red lettering commands attention. A red tablecloth under giftware or plants you want to sell will move them faster. Use red display tables to call attention to items. In a long area such as a greenhouse, store, or display garden, put red at the far end—paint the wall red or plant bright red flowers—and the bright color will visually advance and shorten the distance.

Blue

Blue is a color that calms and also carries great authority. It's a cooling color and often conveys top quality or winners (blue ribbons). How can you use blue?

Blue is a recessive color. If you want to make a garden end or some part of your store look farther away, put blue there. Blue is one of the first colors we lose as day turns to night; it doesn't stand out in dim lighting or in shaded areas, so use blue flowers in partial shade or sun in display gardens, and leave them on top of benches in greenhouses.

Yellow

Our vision works faster for yellow than for other colors. Yellow is associated with cheerfulness, quickness, and being inexpensive. Yellow often portrays new and exciting. It calls our attention to things.

Yellow is a good sale color—it says fast and inexpensive. Put sale items on a yellow table. Use yellow signs to feature special prices. Painting your delivery trucks yellow says "fast delivery" to customers. Because yellow captures our attention quickest, it's a good color around fountains, sculptures, or other special features in display gardens. We can see yellow even in fading light, so it will show up in gardens at night or on lower shelves in garden centers or greenhouses. Yellow is also a good mixer—put it with deep blue, and the combination will appeal to more people than blue alone. The same is true of yellow with dark green or red.

Green

Green is a good color for interiors because it's restful and friendly. It says vitality, security, and stability. And of course, it says money and profit.

Even though green is so closely associated with horticulture, it may not be the best color to use for promoting your business. Studies have shown that we don't take green seriously in business. But don't abandon green—just use it carefully to create a restful atmosphere.

Orange

Orange makes things look affordable. It's often a fad in merchandising and fashion. It's associated with fall and the transition to winter—orange is a transitional color.

Combine orange with dark green to appeal to a wider audience. Use it to say "affordable" in your store. Paint walls and fixtures orange to create a warm, you-can-afford-our-prices atmosphere.

Black and White

These natural opposites have opposite connotations associated with them. White means good, pure, and refined. It's still one of the top-selling house paints. Though black sometimes has negative connotations, it's also authoritative and elegant.

Use the two colors together to convey authority. A black-and-white tile floor in a cut flower area such as for a wedding display lends formality and elegance.

Off the Shelf, November/December 1997.

Sell More Nursery Stock!

Joli A. Shaw

There's more to selling nursery stock than simply lining up trees and shrubs out in the parking lot corral or in the back of the garden center. With a few simple additions and easy display strategies, you can make nursery stock more appealing and easier to buy for your customers. In a recent presentation at the Ohio International Floral Short Course, Debbie Frey of Bailey Nurseries Inc., a St. Paul, Minnesota, grower, offered these tips:

For bare-root stock, use signs with pictures so customers know what plants look like when they're in leaf.

Arrange your displays so customers can serve themselves. Use raised beds, and put plants on benches. Customers will touch, feel, look, and buy more.

Mix different types of plants—you don't have to put only one category together.

Use plants in containers in displays—you don't have to plant plants to make an effective display. A simple, inexpensive way to make an attractive bed: Box in an area with boards or logs, then fill it with dirt or mulch and put in plants.

Don't forget to label the plants you put in display gardens. Use signs beyond just the tag in the pot.

Mix different conifers and nursery stock together for visual appeal. Don't be afraid to combine deciduous plants with evergreens. Just make sure everything is well tagged.

You don't have to display nursery stock in long rows. Use circular displays and winding pathways to provide visual interest and lead customers through the garden center. If you do use long rows, make an interesting mix of plants with lots of pathways and walkways.

Pull height into the display—a lot of low plants is boring. Mix trees and shrubs to add visual interest. Also, it's easy to use ornamental grasses for displays to add texture and variety.

Customers love to shop under structures. Nursery stock doesn't have to be outside. Even if it's just a narrow wood trellis that follows along pathways, it will lead people through your garden center.

Use mass displays of one variety with mature examples of each plant at the end of the bench.

Use hay bales in the fall for displays. Stack them on different levels for variety.

Use unique category signage: "Small-growing plants up to 12 inches tall," "Plants for small gardens," "Plants for autumn and winter color."

Off the Shelf, September/October 1997.

Merchandising Your Cooler

Janice Fleury

You can get more usable merchandising space from your existing floral cooler if you have the right fixtures. Let the vivid colors of the flowers attract shoppers and do the selling for you. A well-designed fixture will utilize and increase merchandising space and provide an attractive, functional display.

Create a Mass of Color

One way to organize and increase the space inside your cooler is to incorporate a bouquet display system. This type of system organizes single stems or bouquets in a colorful array positioned on the back wall of the cooler. Almost every floral cooler can have this system fitted inside. The upright standards are screwed into the wall to support the system. Adjustable brackets in twelve-, fourteen-, sixteen-, and eighteen-inch lengths are provided to give a graduated tiered effect. Telescoping vase racks adjust to your desired width. Two to five vases can be suspended from each rack. You can put a bouquet system behind one or two doors, leaving additional space for predesigned floral arrangements.

A Dramatic, Updated Look

For more merchandising impact and versatility in your cooler, mirrored or gloss-black slatwall can be installed on the back wall or the partition. Use only moisture-proof slatwall specifically designed for cooler interiors. This will ensure that the slatwall does not warp or buckle. Slatwall brackets can be positioned and repositioned in minutes to arrange glass shelving or graduated vase tiers. Slatwall will dramatically update the look of your existing cooler. You can use chrome or black slatwall brackets to complement your slatwall color.

Two Square Feet of Impact

For increased and effective merchandising space outside of your cooler, you may want to use one or more mobile displays for impulse purchases. Position these displays near the cash register, on the outside wide walk (during specific seasonal periods), and in the entryway or any other area that might entice shoppers.

Most units take only twenty-four inches of floor space. When floral stock decreases, mobile displays can be converted from ten to six vases in a few minutes. This will ensure a fuller, more desirable look. Some racks have wheels on the back, making them easy to position and enabling employees to maneuver them like a handcart.

All of the above merchandising ideas can be completed at minimal costs and can be adapted to almost every floral cooler or location. Start using your existing floral cooler and floor space to the maximum, and increase your profits.

Off the Shelf, January/February 1998.

Add European Flair to Your Cut Flower Displays

Tracy Dominick

So you don't have an outdoor flower stand on a cobblestone street or the Eiffel Tower as a backdrop. You can still offer a large assortment of flowers in monochromatic bunches and long cuts, displayed in bronze, copper, and other metal containers to recreate the ambiance of a European cut flower display. With a few simple steps, you can merchandise the European way, and voilà—your sales will soar.

"The keys to a European display are packaging, perceived quality and value-added prices, and the display fixture itself," says Mike Black, Skyline Bouquet, Far Rockaway, New York.

Mike suggests starting with a basic step display, or building a display on top of wooden barrels or crates. A standard ten-inch bucket inside a wicker basket provides an Old World feel, and Mike recommends following the European trend of metal containers and avoiding commercial merchandise fixtures, which can be very uncreative and out of date. Metal cans are available in most home centers—Mike suggests investing in top-quality, no-rust zinc cans imported from Europe, available from Dilpack in Miami, Florida.

Selling your cut flowers in metal containers attracts customers because of the modern simplicity of metal combined with a farmer's market suggestion. "What a European display does is give the customer perceived freshness from the farm," Mike says. Europeans also use oversized bouquets to increase perceived quality.

Color is important in emulating a European display. Techniques such as laterals, ribbon effects, and monochromatic themes are effective eye-catchers. Mike points out that European bouquets are not as mixed as American, and they use straight, monochromatic bunches or nosegays. Lighting your European display with a very soft white light (75 watts) will help bring out the vibrant colors of the flowers.

Mike says a versatile display entices frequent shoppers to buy more. "Most people change [their display] with the seasons, but I recommend that at least every month you reconfigure your display." Even though you may be displaying the same flowers, you can make them look different, especially for your repeat customers. You want them to "buy bouquets and flowers as part of their weekly buying rituals," as the Europeans do. "If they feel like they've already bought something, they won't even come near the display," says Mike. "Here at Skyline Bouquet, we never, ever give the customer the same bouquet twice." They use the same basic recipes but make their bouquets look unique every week by changing the mixes and using different colors and ornamentals such as dahlias and *Celosia.*

Retailers can increase the gross profit margin by about 10% or more by using quality packaging. "Avoid cheap, thin plastic packaging—it has to be thick and crisp," Mike says. Mike's found that a five- or six-cent investment on better packaging raises the retail value of a bouquet by a dollar or more.

Skyline is available for display consulting throughout the Northeast as far north as Canada, as far south as South Carolina, and as far west as Illinois. For more information, call Skyline Bouquet, Far Rockaway, New York, Tel: (718) 634-7000.

Off the Shelf, September/October 1998.

Cutting Gardens: A Different Way to Display and Sell

Shirley Remes

The Heidgen family was looking for something to bring more people into their greenhouse and retail center during late summer and early fall, typically a slower time of year for them. They decided to try a cutting garden.

"Everybody has pumpkins; we wanted to be a little different," said Matt Heidgen, who operates Shady Hill Gardens in Elburn and Batavia, Illinois, in the western suburbs of Chicago, along with his brothers, Joe and Karl, and his father, Chuck.

Several years ago, while at a conference in Seattle, they toured some local growers and noticed one had a cutting garden. This seemed to be something unique in the Chicago area that would draw destination shoppers. Cut flowers are a popular item to buy in supermarkets; why not offer something fresher at a competitive price?

"Many consumers also like the aspect of the you-pick type of shopping, whether it's strawberries, tomatoes, or such. We thought we could tie into that," says Matt.

They began to draw up plans, starting with eight 50-by-4-feet beds at their Elburn site. Matt and his brothers grew some trial varieties, looking for plants that would bloom late in the summer, during the cooler months.

"People don't want to pick flowers standing in the baking sun during the beastly hot months of July and August," he says. After a couple of years of growing a few varieties, experimenting with cutting back and deadheading to delay blooming until the end of summer, they planted up the beds this past summer, starting with annuals. Blue salvia, *Celosia* (plume and cockscomb), *Zinnia,* sunflowers, snapdragons, and asters were among the flowers they planted.

To market the new service, they mentioned it in a fall flyer that went out to about one-third of their mailing list of approximately twenty-thousand customers, choosing zip codes that were closest to their location. They also advertised in two local newspapers.

To decide on a price, they researched local florists and wholesalers and came up with twenty-five cents per stem, with the exception of sunflowers, which were eighty cents. A booth near the cutting gardens holds baskets and shears for shoppers, as well as pricing information. "We were very pleased with the first year; we met our goals," says Matt. Some women scooped up armloads of flowers to take home, delighted with the bargain they were getting.

Most of the flowers put in the original bed were grown from seed as an economy move, as the first effort was experimental. But because sales were good, the Heidgens are doubling the number of beds this year and adding more varieties of annuals and perennials.

"We want sunflowers coming constantly in fall, long-stem snapdragons, more asters, probably *Statice, Cosmos, Gomphrena,* purple coneflowers, black-eyed Susans, Shasta daisies, and *Yarrow.* We may try bulbs—tulips and daffodils in spring, . . . but we're a little leery because they all may bloom at the same time," says Matt, explaining that they want to extend flowers' blooming times so customers have a longer time to shop. The family is also considering growing flowers that customers can use for dried arrangements.

Off the Shelf, January/February 1999.

Doubling Sales, by the Numbers

Quantity pricing is proven to increase sales. But don't use numbers that make it hard for your customers to calculate how much of a deal they're getting. A more effective sign might have read "$2 each or 6 for $11."

Consumers will buy more when given limits on how many of an item they can buy, according to a study by the University of Illinois.

Research conducted in three U.S. cities found that shoppers will buy twice as many of an item if signage gives them a strict limit, such as "Soup—79¢, limit 12 per person." In this example, customers bought an average of seven cans when given a limit, but only three to four cans when signs indicated no limit.

Shoppers also bought 30 percent more of a product when it was priced in multiples—for instance, three for three dollars. Also noted in the study: An item didn't have to be on sale, and the signage didn't even have to give a price—just suggest a number to buy, such as "Buy 18 candy bars for your freezer." When shoppers were presented with such a suggestion, they increased purchases from one to three candy bars.

Consumer Buzz, January/February 1999.

From Clothing to Calendulas

Joli A. Shaw

While shopping recently, it occurred to me that the garden center industry could learn a lot from Gap Inc., the company that owns the Old Navy, Gap, and Banana Republic chains of clothing stores. Each of these stores has become a leader in its category; each has a special blend of merchandising and customer service; yet each targets a completely different market.

Likewise, the floriculture industry has these levels of shopping: We can liken Old Navy to the discounters and big box stores; Gap becomes supermarkets and the typical independent garden center; and Banana Republic is florists and upscale, often urban, independent garden centers. So why not take a lesson from these chains?

Old Navy has proven that you can have trendy merchandising without squandering your profits on it. Their open layout and industrial-type floor-to-ceiling shelves let customers see the product. It's a warehouse look without the warehouse feel. The message: Low priced doesn't have to mean cinder blocks and two-by-fours.

Why not incorporate that look into your lawn-and-garden department? Try wood and metal shelving that can hold palettes of plants. Consumers want to see the colorful products they're buying, and shelving like this provides the perfect venue for it.

Similarly, Gap has made a name for itself for its simplicity. The adjective I most often hear to describe the chain is "classic." Stark white walls, shelving, and display units accented with chrome contrast with light wood floors. Faceless mannequins wear a spotlighted piece of clothing with a table nearby holding that item in three or four colors.

Try this in your garden center: Go with a monochromatic theme to accent and spotlight the flowers and plants you sell—let your product provide the color. Use basic white laminate for functional, durable displays that provide a background for any plant, green or blooming. And hard lines are packaged in increasingly colorful and eye-catching bags and boxes, so let them speak for themselves.

The Banana Republic customer is a bit more discerning, as is the high-end independent garden center or florist shopper. The décor reflects it: glossy wood displays and polished hardwood floors accented with glass shelving and chrome trim. The trendy music plays softly in the background, and potpourri and candles (all for sale) lightly scent the air.

Now I'm not recommending glass shelving for plants because of the constant cleaning you'd be doing after watering, but I do think you could incorporate many of these ideas into your stores to entice your customers to buy more.

A successful retail florist from the Philadelphia area once told me that the key to selling more to his customers is to sell to their senses, and Banana Republic also recognizes this. For sound, they play carefully selected CDs in the store and make sure to offer those CDs for sale at the cash registers. And for added effect, you might look into private labeling for your own CD: What shopper wouldn't want a *Sounds of the Urban Garden* CD?

Another part of the key to Banana Republic's upscale yet inviting atmosphere, a friend of mine is convinced, is the lighting. He says the whole store seems "cream colored," and he's right. Their lighting is designed to spotlight the products, yet still provide a warm feel. You can do the same in your store with carefully placed track lighting and built-in can lights.

Ideas like these are everywhere, so use them!

In My Opinion, March/April 1999.

Chapter 11
To Everything a Season

Holiday Horticulture

George Ball Jr.

An amazing number of plants have become an extremely important part of the holiday seasons. Examples include the pumpkin, gourd, corn stalk, and chrysanthemum for Thanksgiving; mistletoe, cyclamen, holly, and poinsettia for Christmas; lily, palm frond, and narcissus for Easter. In addition to the popular holidays, others have become more secular than religious, such as St. Valentine's Day, when a man gives his beloved a rose, and Halloween, which is celebrated today with more than mere carved pumpkins. In the last few years, black- and orange-colored pansies and Indian corn have joined the spookfest. The garden shop offers savvy retailers a great opportunity to celebrate the seasons year-round with their customers.

Four seasonal periods occur, more or less distinctly, throughout North America. Plants smooth these transitions as well as help us mark the important occasions—remembrances of the lives we share with family, neighbors, and friends. Plants should be sold in the same spirit!

What's the Future of the Holidays?

Thanksgiving, Christmas, Mother's Day, Memorial Day—they're all going to become vastly more important for two main reasons. First, the aging of the baby boomers will supply garden retailers with an enormous number of potential customers who will be asking for both nostalgia and new plant-related material to help them celebrate their home lives. Consumer research clearly indicates that as boomers age, they act out high-energy activities and increase more relaxing and contemplative pursuits, such as house decorating.

In addition, the boomers' familiar predisposition toward innovative expressions of tradition will find its outlet in creative new holiday plants. This is what makes Martha Stewart's succulent wreath—unimaginable a decade ago—so appealing. It's the BMW of holiday door décor.

However, fashions pass and give way to periodic revivals of so-called old-fashioned traditions—the old reliables. Who hasn't been confronted at a holiday party by a proud hostess with a cup of muddy cider that she proclaims is filled with seasonal spices and then "mulled"? Some of the words even have an heirloom quality.

But keep in mind the real bottom line of the holidays: Traditionally, they're expressions of sensual delights, and people love them. The sights, sounds, and aromas of Christmas are extremely familiar. They evoke fond memories of holidays past. More can be done—tastefully—with Easter, the principal Christian holiday.

Take opportunities to celebrate the many ethnic celebrations that occur in many communities. Look for cross-promotional opportunities with your stores' candy and food departments. I'll never forget the Czech ladies who stuffed and glazed apricots, then sold them in the aisles of my local supermarket during the winter holidays when I was young and living in Chicago's Albany Park neighborhood. Think of the festival costumes of the central, eastern and southern European communities, whose immigrants are pouring into urban and suburban communities and moving up the economic ladder. These folks already love plants, as they come from the "garden of Europe." They'll be touched by your thoughtfulness. Nothing is quite as effective as word-of-mouth advertising, especially in traditional ethnic communities.

Happy Holidays!

George, January/February 1998.

Festive Flowers for Jewish Holidays

The traditional Jewish holidays, while not associated with a floral icon as recognizable as the poinsettia or Easter lily, are important sales opportunities for any floral outlet wanting to serve every member of its customer base.

Frank Laning, owner of Flowers by Frank Laning, in Chappaqua, New York, does a booming business serving the flower needs of his predominately Jewish clientele.

"We probably do a bigger Passover business than we do Easter," Frank says. The spring holiday of Passover is the festival of freedom, commemorating the Exodus, and is one of the main flower-giving holidays of the Jewish faith. In some markets blue and white flowers, representing the colors of the Israeli flag, are popular. However, like any high-end clientele, Frank's customers prefer flowers that complement their décor, so any color or variety may be used, "just like the nontraditionalist at Christmas doesn't want red and green." Many also provide their own containers, which may be family heirlooms or contemporary pieces.

For Christmas and Hanukkah, Frank's customers often do a "non-Christmas" Christmas that doesn't "scream" red and green, but instead uses a wide range of

Red, gold, brown, and orange flowers and foliage help Jews greet their new year on Rosh Hashanah.

flowers and lots of Christmas greens and garlands. "We just call them holiday decorations." Customers might specify white and blue for a Hanukkah party.

The Jewish New Year, Rosh Hashanah, falls in September and is another important flower-giving holiday. Fall colors predominate. Ten days later is Yom Kippur, the Day of Atonement, a solemn holiday in which the temples are decorated with white flowers, signifying purity.

Probably the best reason for Jews to buy flowers is the weekly observation of the Sabbath, which begins every Friday at sundown and continues until Saturday at sundown. Frank says many of his customers have standing weekly orders.

Jewish Holidays

Rosh Hashanah	September	Fall colors
Yom Kippur	Ten days after Rosh Hashanah	White flowers
Hanukkah	December	Blue, white (in some areas)
Passover	Spring	Blue, white, and any flower color
Shavuos (which means "weeks")	Seven weeks after Passover	Flowers, "firstfruits", winter wheat
The Sabbath	Every week	Any flowers

Consumer Buzz, July/August 1999.

Valentine's Day

Valentine's Day Cut Flower Success

Floriculture's No. 1 sales holiday is fast approaching, and consumers' expectations are never higher than on Valentine's Day. Keep your cut flowers and fillers looking great under your customers' scrutiny with these simple tips from the California Cut Flower Commission's *Cut Flower Guide.*

Rose

Some varieties of this Valentine's Day standard are sensitive to ethylene, and exposure may cause bent neck and wilting. To prevent this, unpack your shipments immediately. Place plants in a hydrating solution for about an hour, then transfer to flower food solution. Store in a cooler at 80 to 90 percent humidity for several hours. Vase life is four to twelve days, depending on the variety.

Carnation

Whether you're selling standard carnations, mini carnations, or spray carnations, you'll want to watch these plants' exposure to ethylene. Be sure to hydrate them and store them at 36 to 38°F. Vase life can be one to two weeks or more.

Gypsophila

Commonly known as baby's breath, gypsophila is sensitive to both ethylene and water stress. To avoid stem blockage, cut stems under water, keep buckets clean, and add flower food. Store at 36 to 38°F. Gypsophila can last for seven to ten days, and it has the added bonus of drying well.

Greens

For commonly used greens such as asparagus fern, sprengeri fern, plumosus fern, and leatherleaf fern, your first priority should be hydration—give them lots of water and high humidity. Store the ferns at 38 to 45°F and eucalyptus at 36 to 40°F. Vase life can be one to three weeks or more, depending on variety.

Off the Shelf, January/February 1998.

Take Valentine's Merchandising to Heart

Chris Beytes

Consider a young man buying three Valentine's Day gifts: one for his grandmother who's in a nursing home, one for his sister who's away at college, and one for his girlfriend with whom he hopes to spend a romantic Valentine's evening. He'll have no problem picking out greeting cards; they range from sappy to silly to spicy.

But what about flower gifts? Are you offering him ideas and products that meet the three different emotions he wants to convey? And what about the very diverse needs of all of your other Valentine's Day customers? Here are some ideas to fine-tune your holiday offerings and expand your sales.

A Menu Makes It Easy

The first floral holiday of the year is one of the biggest for floriculture. According to the American Floral Endowment Consumer Tracking Study, Valentine's Day is the No. 3 flower and plant holiday by dollar volume for the year, at 22 percent, behind Christmas (30 percent) and Mother's Day (25 percent). When it comes to just cut flowers, Valentine's Day is No. 1 in both dollar volume (39 percent) and the total number of transactions (36 percent). In fact, it's the No. 1 holiday for florists.

That's part of the problem. With Valentine's Day being basically a one-day holiday, you're often too busy to provide more than just the most basic arrangements and plant upgrades. Your customers are also busy, and the lure of a quick shopping trip through a catalog or the Internet can be strong competition.

"People will trade money for time," says Bobbi Ecker, owner of The FloraPros, a Chicago-area marketing company that specializes in the floriculture industry. Saving time is one reason catalog and Internet sales have boomed. To combat that competition and make Valentine's Day easier for you and your customers, Bobbi suggests that you develop a menu of products that targets a variety of customer needs at several price points.

Naturally, you have to have long-stemmed red roses by the dozen for those customers who won't settle for anything else. But you should also offer unusual alternatives, such as a compact bowl of roses, which makes a very nice centerpiece and lasts longer than long-stemmed roses. You can do the same with carnations. Cross-merchandise with candy, wine, champagne, or gourmet food—perhaps an herb planter with packaged pasta and sauce for a romantic Valentine's Day dinner.

A simple ivy topiary can become a romantic Valentine's Day gift with the addition of a bottle of champagne. Adding cut flowers can alter the degree of romance expressed.

Merchandise your store conveniently: Don't put your arrangements away in the cooler where customers may be afraid to browse. Bring your products out where people can see them up close.

And expand your holiday hours—open earlier and stay open later. We're no longer a nine-to-five society; your business shouldn't be, either.

Color

Red is *the* Valentine's Day color, but that may well be because of who's doing the buying: men. According to a Society of American Florists survey, 37 percent of women say they'd like to receive pastel-colored flowers—pink, yellow, or peach—for Valentine's Day. Red is first choice of 36 percent of women. But red is No. 1 for nearly half of the men surveyed, with pastels coming in third place behind bright colors such as orange, purple, and fuchsia.

Help your male customers understand the feelings and emotions that can be expressed with colors other than red, and have examples on hand. To keep it simple and guarantee availability, advertise "pastel" roses or other flowers rather than specific colors.

The colors and textures of accessories and add-ons also convey emotion. Metallic or black wraps and ribbons express sophistication and elegance, while soft colors or earthy textures have a casual, back-to-nature feel. Use both to offer the same product, whether roses or pot azaleas, in a variety of styles to suit a variety of customer needs.

Specials Make the Day Special

Valentine's Day has a reputation for being expensive. Change that by offering specials, discounts, or deals. It's a way to attract customers and separate yourself from the competition. Have plenty of the specials on hand, but have your employees prepared to sell your customers up a notch or two in price. If they're getting a good price, they may wind up buying more.

One clever idea from Bobbi: Offer a "Valentine's Day all year long" package: an arrangement or plant they take with them and a gift certificate good for another arrangement or plant every month for six months or a year. You can even sweeten the deal by offering the first product free.

Some Grand Larceny

Bobbi offers one important key to remember about Valentine's Day and every holiday, for that matter: "You're not selling flowers and plants; you're selling feelings." The young man above doesn't want flowers; he wants to tell Grandma that he loves her, to tell Sis that he misses her, and tell his sweetheart that he loves her. So you've got to tell him what he can buy to convey those emotions. The best way to do that is with creative signage.

Catalogs are a perfect place to steal catchy marketing phrases that express emotions, says Bobbi. (That's where she gets some of her best ideas.) Catalog copywriters are masters of expressing in writing the emotions they want their products to represent. It's easy to change a few words and come up with creative ideas for marketing flowers and plants. Here are some examples Bobbi pulled from a recent catalog:

- "It's the career fashion of the season" can be changed to "It's the flower fashion of the season."
- "The easy feel and great look of denim" can be changed to "The easy feel and great look of carnations" (or any other flower).

- "Luxury is back in fashion" can be changed to "Carnations [or any other product] are back in fashion."
- "The season's hottest separates" can be changed to "It's the Valentine's season's hottest look."

You can come up with phrases that suit a particular product. Roses are "elegant," "spectacular," "sensational." They "melt the heart." Potted plants can "keep your love growing." A mixed planter of herbs can be "the fragrance of love." Pull your employees together and brainstorm! Try different catalogs for different emotions. Try Victoria's Secret for sexy themes.

Once you've developed marketing themes for your products, try selling by the results your customer can expect rather than by the number of flowers or the price. One rose can express love as well as a dozen, if merchandised and packaged creatively. And it's a way to break away from the "How much is a dozen roses?" game.

Consumer Buzz, January/February 1998.

Reaching the Hearts of Teens

Chris Beytes

Are teenagers in the market for Valentine's Day flowers? Or are they too wrapped up in the latest lip gloss, CDs, or video games to care?

"Teenage girls love to receive flowers," answers Carole Braden, senior editor with *Seventeen* magazine. With a circulation of 2.4 million, *Seventeen* reportedly reaches one out of every two female teenagers in America, and the magazine is closely tapped into what motivates them. Carole adds that a high percentage of teenage boys say they'd love to receive flowers from a girl. How can you tap into this market?

Give Them Value and Style

Teenagers may not be your biggest customer base, but they probably take flower shopping very seriously.

"I would bet that for young people, flowers are not really an impulse buy like they are for a lot of adults," Carole speculates. "They buy them as gifts, and I think that they really plan when it comes to giving a gift for Valentine's

Day or a birthday. They think ahead, and I think that it's sort of an agonizing decision—they want to make sure that they get the perfect thing."

However, teens want value for their hard-earned dollars. "Teenagers have money to spend; a huge percentage of them have jobs now," Carole says. "But they still don't have a ton of disposable income. . . . So I think something that's a good deal would attract them.

"Long-stem roses are notorious for going way up in price for Valentine's Day," she notes. "That might be off-putting to a younger person. However, every teenage girl wants red roses for Valentine's Day."

Along with value, teens want to be treated as adults. "Teenagers now consider themselves sophisticated. They want to feel sophisticated, and they want adults to think that they're sophisticated," Carole says.

With that in mind, "cutesy" arrangements accessorized with teddy bears, Beanie Babies, or balloons might not go over as well with older teenagers. Cross-merchandising ideas could include the coolest new products such as Hard Candy cosmetics or music CDs from popular musicians such as the Backstreet Boys.

Another product idea: "Why not try marketing Valentine's Day to the people who are not in love?" Carole suggests. "A huge portion of our readers don't have boyfriends."

She suggests products marketed to parents to give to daughters, or for girls to give to their fathers or to friends. Valentine's Day "is a nice holiday to just express love and to give gifts to people whom you care about. And I think that's something that [teenage] girls would really get into."

Consumer Buzz, January/February 1999.

Mother's Day

Making the Most of Mother's Day

Want to make sure that Mother's Day is the best it can be? Try these tips from Mary Anne Hansan, vice president of marketing for the Society of American Florists, as published in SAF's *Floral Trend Tracker.*

Reach your loyal customers. Mary suggests calling or mailing last year's Mother Day customers with a friendly holiday reminder. Reward loyal customers by giving them preferred treatment, such as a sneak preview of holiday stock. Also, reward early ordering. Consider starting an electronic frequent-purchase program that can be tracked by phone number in your computer to give customers the incentive to return.

Make Mother's Day shopping easy—consider setting up extra checkout lines during busy times, such as this outdoor checkout area at Flowerwood Nursery, Crystal Lake, Illinois.

Target women customers. Avoid advertisements that use negative comparisons—they turn women off, Mary says. Instead, create marketing messages that center on family happiness, a primary motivation behind floral purchasing. And consider cause-related promotions that support women's health programs, children, shelters, arts, or conservation.

Make shopping easy. Invite your VIP customers to a "fast and easy" Mother's Day preview—their responses could be a good indication of hot items to stock up on for the holiday. Keep the holiday stress-free for customers and staff: Set up extra checkouts as the holiday approaches. Also, add extra phone lines. Make sure your staff is thoroughly trained and empowered to prevent delays. If possible, you might consider a drive-through with a limited menu of gift options. And offer extended hours during Mother's Day week—you might even open up on Mother's Day and pick up some extra business!

Make sure your displays grab attention. Arrange theme displays—by color, collectible, or decorating style. Provide informative signage.

Appeal to gardeners. A selection of artfully arranged planters or window boxes is a good way to officially launch your summer garden season. They also give women an incentive to come into your store. And Mother's Day gives them an excuse to buy!

Don't forget the men. Men are 35 percent of your Mother's Day business, Mary says, and they buy to look good to their wives and mothers. Assure them that they won't go wrong by purchasing a gift from your store.

Consumer Buzz, March/April 1998.

Fall & Halloween

Beyond Mums: Fall Merchandising Tips

Joli A. Shaw

Unusual annuals such as *Scaevola* and *Brachycome* are the rage to spice up spring sales, but what do you do for the second season—fall? Retailers typically stick with standbys such as garden mums and, in the South, pansies, but there's a whole selection of cool-weather crops that you can take advantage of to increase sales. Try ornamental kale, asters, violas, Proven Winners' Fall Magic series, or colorful fall-hued foliage plants such as *Croton*.

Marketing and merchandising are the keys to success with the fall season—you have to tell your customers what to do with these "new" crops. Breeders recognize this and increasingly are offering eye-catching POP materials with their products. Here's a peek at some of the latest marketing packages available and a look at how some of the country's top retailers are taking advantage of the second season.

Ornamental Kale

Despite ornamental kale's excellent fit as a fall plant—it combines well with fall annuals, has outstanding leaf color and shape, and loves cool weather—many consumers don't know what it is. Make it and its benefits known to your customers with striking color bowls and display plantings. Sun-loving kale's colors intensify in cool weather. Tell your customers about it with signage and POP. On Long Island, this colorful wonder has become almost commonplace thanks to top retailers such as Martin Viette's and Hicks. It can be found almost year-round in city plantings, on street corners, and in front yards, says Fred Hicks.

Halloween Displays

By some estimates, Halloween is now one of the five most lucrative holidays for retailers, and in some areas it is second only to Christmas sales. Take advantage of consumers' yen for the eerie with clever displays like this one at Wannemaker's, Downer's Grove, Illinois. Here, they've used faux tombstones with catchy epitaphs—"Here lies Buck Naked—died of exposure"—combined with garden mums, ornamental grasses, shrubs, and even statuary. Fall is so popular at Wannemaker's that they've decided to start a fall garden show to capitalize on it, says Jim Wannemaker. The show will feature mums, pumpkins, perennials, and pansies, along with their full line of Halloween items, all displayed with the Wannemaker's trademark flair for display. "You have to show what the plants would look like [in the garden] instead of just putting them on the shelf," says Jim. "Make a miniyard so you can show customers how everything would look in their yard."

Container Foliage Plants

Recognizing fall season possibilities, Proven Winners recently introduced a line of foliage plants specifically for fall hanging baskets and containers. The Fall Magic collection includes varieties in reds, golds, purples, silvers, browns, and greens that can be combined with mums, asters, pansies, and other crops for striking arrangements. This year they've added four varieties, which can be ordered individually. Point-of-purchase materials are also available. Labels resemble a maple leaf and include growing tips; corrugated plastic signs feature shots of the collection in plantings.

Pansies

Capitalizing on the Halloween trend, PanAmerican Seed has introduced three new pansies that make fall merchandising easy. The Trick or Treat Mix combines black shades, orange, and orange with face; Purple Jester features purple blooms with white faces; Halloween has dramatic black flowers. Each has a compact habit and medium-sized blooms. Merchandise them alone or as a collection in black or orange containers for Halloween, or combine them with other fall staples in color bowls or hanging baskets.

Mums

Mums are the quintessential fall crop, but that doesn't mean they have to be boring. Send your customers through a "sea of mums" as they come up the walkway to your garden center by mixing bright colors and pot sizes. Combine them with other fall favorites such as ornamental grasses and perennials in different heights and containers for visual interest. Remember to make it easy for consumers to grab the plant they want by creating curved walkways—not just straight rows—to weave through as they shop your displays.

Sunflowers

One of the most sure-fire ways to attract consumers to your displays is to incorporate current trends into them. For example, Connecticut Cut Flower, Bantam, Connecticut, combines giant sunflowers, seen on everything from wallpaper and kitchen towels to clothing and accessories, with a variety of fall crops. The colors they use—bronze, orange, yellow, and deep plum—reflect fall and give consumers a feel for the season. Crops used in their display include regular and miniature pumpkins, mums, flowering kale, and sunflowers.

Croton

Fall displays don't have to use only orange and brown. Try something nontraditional, like this display, which is based around *Croton*'s brilliant orange, red, and yellow colors. It combines *Croton* with red, yellow, and bronze flowering plants such as mums and *Kalanchoe*, and throws in turquoise and metallic gold pot covers for visual interest.

Second-Season Marketing

For a targeted promotion with specific Midwestern growers and retailers, Novartis has created a Second Season Pansy tag designed to promote pansies for their over-wintering ability and cool-weather appeal. "The intention of the program is to alert consumers to something that they're not aware of—not the color of the pansy, but that this is a second-season product," says Meredith Shank, Novartis's marketing communications manager. The tagline "Made to survive winter and thrive again in spring" appears on each tag along with a penguin. Novartis has targeted the program to include pansy varieties that are genetically strongest for overwintering, Meredith says. Tags go on their Sky and Delta series. On the back of each tag are planting instructions and a guarantee for satisfaction. Novartis provides a full refund if the customer sends proof of purchase to them, and Meredith says they've received a scant five returns per year since the program's inception.

Fall Festivals

Fall festivals are a great way to increase traffic during what can be a slower season. Scheduling events such as hayrides, apple bobbing, scarecrow-making contests, or pumpkin decorating for children is a sure draw for today's top gardeners—the Baby Boomers. Some experts estimate that children wield $160 billion to $400 billion in purchasing influence as parents turn to children for buying advice. Use that potential to your advantage.

GrowerTalks, May 1998.

The Ultimate Pansy Sale

Joli A. Shaw

How would you like to have one October day in your retail store with sales one and a half times your best spring sales day? Alice Longfellow, Longfellow's Garden Center, Centertown, Missouri, has done that and more with her Pansy Festival, an annual event designed to increase sales and to develop customer loyalty.

Alice started the Pansy Festival, held each year in mid-October, six years ago to promote sales in a slow time of the year. "Pansies were something that weren't going to go anywhere in my area if I didn't get behind them and promote them," says Alice. "People in our area are very conservative—I knew they wouldn't grow things in the fall. Once they tried them, they couldn't believe how great they were."

And how. Gardeners travel from miles around to come to Longfellow's, which is ten miles from the nearest town. The Pansy Festival has become an event people plan their schedules around. On one Sunday during the festival, Alice counted 160 cars in the parking lot.

And who could blame them, with the myriad activities the festival offers? Each year, Alice tries to provide three to four different events for customers: clowns, face painting, pumpkin painting, hayrides, caricatures, a coloring contest, a duck pond. Alice is targeting return customers, and she's doing that by targeting their kids.

In addition, Alice invites local nonprofit groups to sell food such as barbecue and funnel cakes. This not only keeps the customers happy, it also shows she's giving something to the community.

As part of the Pansy Festival, customers have the opportunity to redeem "Pansy Dollars," which they can earn throughout the year and are given away based on the amount of the purchase—one Pansy Dollar for every ten dollars purchased.

Match one Pansy Dollar with one U.S. dollar, and you get 50% off. "The customer perceives it as a 50 percent off sale, but you have to spend money to get it," says Alice. "What it actually is is an 8 percent sale, but not all of the Pansy Dollars come back, so you're looking realistically at a 3 percent sale."

Because Pansy Dollars aren't dated, customers can save them from year to year. Customers accumulate the Pansy Dollars during the year and spend them during the October festival—one person brought in more than six hundred Pansy Dollars! "Think about that—they had to have spent over six thousand dollars!" Alice says. "It's a way for us to say, 'We appreciate your business.'"

Even with these profits, Alice cautions that retailers considering a similar promotion think about all angles of the festival. "You have a lot of very large crowds. That creates confusion, potential shoplifting, accidents, and mistakes." And an event like this takes planning, she says. "You have to be highly organized, and you need a lot of space. What about parking? What if you have bad weather?"

Still, for Alice, the potential problems are outweighed by the end profits—her sales continue to increase, and the Pansy Festival continues to increase business.

GrowerTalks, *May 1998.*

Fall—It's Not Just for Pansies Anymore

Teresa Aimone

As you read this, bedding plant season is here. Your well-organized, well-maintained displays of products are a big hit with your customers, and it's all you can do to keep your sales area stocked. Your customers are thrilled and are pledging their undying shopping loyalty to your store. Sound familiar? Sound close? Well, we hope that's true because that means they'll be coming back for fall plants.

You've heard the slogan Fall Is for Planting. That's true. Fall is the time to plant trees and shrubs, pansies, and garden mums. It's also the time to plant asters, dahlias, dianthus, ornamental cabbage and kale, and snapdragons. Are these the plants that come to mind when you hear the phrase "fall plants"? Or are garden mums and pansies all you dare to offer after Labor Day?

There's nothing like a mass of colorful garden mums to stop traffic in the fall, such as this display at Walnut Hill Greenhouse in Connecticut. But don't ignore all the great plants that complement them.

Please don't ignore garden mums and pansies; they are products your customers are familiar with and that make them feel successful when they garden. And don't flood your retail area with all of these different products listed below. But there is no reason why you shouldn't consider being the innovator in your area and at least letting your customers (and you) be more creative. Part of the beauty of these products is that they aren't really new—most have been around for a while. Their value and performance have been tested and proven garden-worthy. Depending on the region of the country, some will perform as annuals, others as perennials. So let your displays take on a new look for fall with these "seasoned" garden veterans: asters, dahlias, dianthus, ornamental cabbage and kale, and snapdragons.

A Is for Asters

The daisylike flowers of asters are familiar to many gardeners. Flower colors include blue, violet, purple, pink, red, and white, all with purple/black or yellow centers. Asters come in annual and perennial forms. The annual form, China aster, actually belongs in a different genus than the perennial type. Perennial asters are also called Michaelmas daisies or New York asters. Plants purchased in four-inch or larger containers establish faster and flower better for your customers. If possible, bring plants in around mid to late August to extend the flowering season. Tell your customers to plant asters in full sun or partial shade. If you sell plants for "specialty gardens," recommend taller varieties of asters for cut flowers.

Dynamic Dahlias

Like asters, dahlias have a familiar face, yet that face comes in a great variety of forms and colors. Dahlias have a long flowering season from late spring until late fall and can be started from seed, cuttings, or tubers. The variety of flower forms, colors (everything except blue), and plant height make dahlias an extremely adaptable plant for retail sales. Most of the shorter varieties are seed grown; these can be sold in packs and four-inch pots. Mid-sized varieties can be used as florist-quality pot plants with upscale market packaging. Market larger varieties in six-inch or larger containers.

All dahlias will form tubers by late fall. Your customers can dig up the tubers at the end of the season, place them in a cool, dry place, and plant them again in the spring. These same successful gardeners will be back for more next year! Dahlias like warm, sunny locations sheltered from strong winds and planted in well-fertilized, well-drained soil.

The Diversity of Dianthus

Dianthus are normally grown as annuals, although some varieties will act as biennials or perennials. This diverse group of plants includes small border plants and groundcovers, as well as the florist's carnation. Earlier dianthus breeding produced more fragrant varieties, although some of the newer varieties offered today can also be marketed as fragrant. Bring dianthus into your retail area a little later in the season to take advantage of the bright sunny days and cooler nights that dianthus love. Plants can be grown in packs or pots, but those plants grown in pots should perform best for fall gardens. Dianthus like sunny locations and well-drained, slightly alkaline soil.

They come in a wide range of colors (except blue, but breeders are working on this one), as well as a combination of colors and different flower forms.

What Are These?

This is a typical reaction when customers first see ornamental kale. You, as a retailer, need to quickly learn the basics of this plant because sales of ornamental kale are growing by leaps and bounds. Why? They're effortless for gardeners to grow; they have outstanding leaf color and shape; they combine well with fall annuals; and they last a long time in the garden. Plus, they're just unusual.

"What are these?" will usually be followed by "I'll take a dozen!" when you show your customers how to use flowering kale. All forms of kale offer stupendous color and durability until the snow falls.

Technically, ornamental cabbage and kale are both kales. Ornamental cabbage is called so because of its rounded, cabbagelike leaves; what is typically referred to as kale has fringed leaves. Also available is a feather-leafed type of kale that grows taller than other kale and cabbage. All are edible, although a bit more bitter than the traditional vegetable types. When sold at retail, plants will have lightly colored center leaves—pink, purple, red, or white. As temperatures cool, these colors greatly intensify; this is what makes them so ideal for fall plantings. The cooler it is, the brighter and better they look. Plants should be grown in full sun in the garden. You can buy them in four-inch (minimum size container) and larger. Gallon-sized plants are commonly grown.

Try to avoid plants that have yellow lower leaves or look like they have a "stalk" or stem—not a great sight at retail. Your customers can plant them up to the base of the lowest set of leaves, and they'll perform just fine, but try to avoid buying these simply because they look unappealing. And if your customers don't know how to plant them correctly, kale will lose much of their garden appeal.

If you're in the South, where kale blooms all winter long, you'll get an added bonus. When the weather warms up, the plants will "bolt," just like the vegetable forms of cabbage and kale will. Plants will grow into twelve-inch-plus cone-shaped plants topped with small yellow flowers for a little added drama. There are even cut flower varieties—what more could you ask for?

A Familiar Favorite

There aren't many gardeners who don't recognize snapdragons. Pinching the flower's sides makes the dragon's mouth open, then close back with a snap. Along with this familiar flower form, breeding efforts have also produced open-faced butterfly types as well as double-flowered azalea snapdragons. Along with three flower forms, snapdragons are also available as dwarf (six to eight inches tall); medium (ten to fourteen inches); and tall (fourteen inches and up). These colorful annuals can be marketed as plants for borders, backgrounds, cut flowers, or butterfly and bee gardens.

Like dianthus, fall offers the perfect opportunity for snapdragons to shine under the season's bright days and cooler nights. To obtain the longest bloom season, try to purchase plants that are just coming into flower. Encourage customers to remove spent flowers so plants will continue to bloom. Snapdragons do well in sunny locations; taller varieties should be staked.

Customers Don't Like Surprises

Customers like to know what they are getting for their money; they don't want to bring something home and have it perform differently than promised. They also don't want to play guessing games at the retail outlet, so let them know what they're buying and what to do with it when they get it home. Signs, POP material, gardening tips, and picture tags will familiarize your customers with these fall plants.

Be Nice

Steaming asphalt isn't the best place to display bedding plants, nor are areas beyond the reach of the watering hose. Unfortunately, it isn't uncommon to see this happen, and there are times when these measures are unavoidable. But when plants arrive, water them (unless they are soaking wet), remove any dead foliage and flowers, and place them in their appropriate sun/shade display area by the corresponding signage or POP material. Try to give them the best treatment possible. Providing the best environment for your product ensures your customers that they'll get the gardening results they want and deserve.

May/June 1998.

Keeping the Fun in Fall Cut Flowers

Chris Beytes

With its traditional earthy, muted colors, fall can be a somber time of year for flower merchandising if we get carried away with the brown, rust, and gold themes. Instead, keep the fun in fall by emphasizing bright colors such as yellows and purples, suggests Highland Supply's Julie Wilkinson, director of creative marketing.

"Purple is almost synonymous with black and orange for Halloween now and has been for some years since Hallmark started featuring it," Julie says. "I've noticed that it's grown and grown over the years." Julie says she expects to see additional cut flower packers including more and more purple into their mixes, as cut flowers, picks, or dried materials. "[Purple] has become a traditional color in a very short time."

Also for Halloween, there are plenty of wraps and sleeves printed with traditional Halloween motifs, such as Highland's new Ghosts & Goblins, a roll film featuring a busy pattern of Halloween elements.

One you get into the more traditional, formal season of Thanksgiving, you can bring out the earth tones. Julie says clear wraps and sleeves are very popular. These allow embellishments such as dried plant material or picks of dried pods to be featured without a pattern interfering. Highland also offers a film sleeve in an autumn leaf pattern. Printed with mottled ink, it gives more interest to the colors.

Off the Shelf, July/August 1998.

Take the Hollow out of Halloween

Joli A. Shaw

Retail analysts everywhere are reporting on Halloween's amazing sales increases in recent years. So why, I thought, aren't garden centers taking advantage of consumers' apparent affection for the spooky, scary, orange-and-black-themed holiday?

However, before I could editorialize on the topic, Alvi Voight, Pennsylvania State University professor emeritus, addressed precisely that subject in his Flower Marketing Information *newsletter. As Alvi is one of the premier agricultural economists in the country, I defer to his expertise. He has graciously agreed to let us reprint a portion of his editorial:*

In making one of our short, very infrequent visits to one of our town's (State College, Pennsylvania) mass marketers, curiosity always attracts a peek at the garden center. . . . Near the doorway from inside of the garden center to the outside product area there was a container of Halloween flower bouquets.

The bouquets were impressive in colorful sleeves with white ghosts, orange moons, black bats, haunted houses/fences, and the words "Boo!" and "Trick or Treat" scattered over the sleeve. We purchased an eight-stem bouquet priced at $2.97 and consisting of three stems of pompons (two yellow, one white), two stems of standard carns, one mini carn stem, and two stems of filler flowers.

Then, two days after our shopping trip, our local newspaper, the *Centre Daily Times,* carried a story indicating U.S. Halloween retail sales were expected to reach $2.5 billion. Depending on the source, Halloween season now ranks as one of the five most lucrative for retailers, and in some sectors is second only to Christmas for product sales. Gets your attention? . . .

Store-bought costumes, plastic pumpkins, makeup, special effects, electronics, plus home decorations which, today, rival Christmas items for retail positioning, generate gigantic Halloween sales. Chocolate sales soar. Manufacturers target consumers of all ages. . . . Halloween has become important because, just like Easter and Christmas, we're seeing a season that now lasts up to a month beforehand and about a week later.

In the *Wall Street Journal,* October same-store sales climbed 4.5 percent, according to an index of major retailers compiled by Goldman, Sachs & Co. The growth was stronger than the 3.3 percent recorded for October 1996. Discount chains led the pack with strong gainers' Wal-Mart and Dayton Hudson up about 6 percent.

The American Floral Endowment's consumer tracking data identified calendar flower-buying occasions and noncalendar flower-buying occasions. Calendar occasions were 19.7 percent. Of that: Christmas/Hanukkah had 6.6 percent; Mother's Day, 4.6 percent; Valentine's Day, 3.9 percent; Easter/Passover, 2.8 percent; Thanksgiving, 0.7 percent and Secretary's Day, 0.3 percent. Father's Day and Halloween were tied for seventh with just 0.2 percent.

Is our flower industry missing out on a hot, up-and-coming Halloween season? Our mass marketer didn't advertise the bouquets. Could our store have sold many more Halloween promo bouquets if they were positioned at the entrance of the store or at the checkouts? Where would they get the necessary supply? If they or other chains were able to get a sufficient supply and were committed and serious about merchandising flowers, what would happen to per capita consumption of flowers? We have an increasing population with increasing income (ability to buy). But we haven't gotten our population's attention, interest, and desire that would (with the ability/income) translate into strong flower sales for Halloween.

In My Opinion, March/April 1998.

Christmas

The Scents of Winter

Go beyond poinsettias and take advantage of consumers' need for color and life during the long, dark days of winter. Pot plants with strong fragrances not only brighten up homes, but they also make great gifts during the holidays. A few to try:

- Paperwhite narcissus, which offers fragrant white flowers
- *Exacum,* or Persian violet, which has a delicate, distinctive smell and small, blue flowers

- *Jasminum polyanthum*, one of the most aromatic of winter pot plants, has an intense fragrance
- Gardenia, of which the most popular is the everblooming gardenia, which has double white, strongly scented flowers
- Dwarf orange (calamondin) or ponderosa lemon, which offers the sweet scent of orange blossoms

Off the Shelf, September/October 1998.

Price Isn't Everything

Joli A. Shaw

For the past few years, retail and wholesale poinsettia prices have been so low that garden centers and producers were happy with a margin as small as just one to five cents. Used as loss leaders by many mass merchandisers and increasingly even independents, these once-premium plants are now commodities in a market where price is the singlemost important character-istic for both the retailer and the consumer. But does it have to be that way?

In the past, the typical poinsettia was eighteen to twenty inches tall, with six to eight large blooms in a 6½-inch to 7-inch pot. Today's average poin-settia, at fourteen to eighteen inches tall, with three to five blooms in a 5½-inch to 6½-inch pot, is only a vague memory of these premium plants. Throughout the distribution chain, we see poinsettias crammed together on shelves and greenhouse benches, their bracts bent and their growth stunted as light and space is limited.

To be sure, plant postharvest, or shelf life, time is shortened as well. Poinsettias grown with less space between them and displayed in sleeves or boxes and not watered are doomed to short lives. The real question is not where the fault lies, but what does the consumer think?

Does the consumer think poinsettias just don't keep like they used to, or is she simply turning to silk replicas in the home decor department to ensure that the table centerpieces she puts out before her party aren't wilted and bractless when the night comes to a close?

And are consumers really looking for the lowest priced poinsettia they can find? I don't think so. They're looking for a pretty plant to brighten their houses during a dark winter. And as some industry members are finding out, they'll pay for it. In a price point test last December, breeder Paul Ecke Ranch, Encinitas, California, asked supermarkets selling 6½-inch premium poinsettias and standard 6-inch pinched poinsettias to price the premiums four dollars higher. Guess what? Consumers overwhelmingly preferred the premium plants. Their larger flowers and additional color were huge draws despite the four-dollar price jump.

You'll probably always have to carry those six-inch pinched plants, but they don't have to make up your entire selection. When you're placing your order for next Christmas, why not ask your vendor about some larger, premium items to try out on your customers? Several stores in the Paul Ecke Ranch experiment say they have the potential to increase sales by 50 percent this year by stocking premium items.

Another bonus with premium plants: They differentiate you from your competition. Ask for different containers and plant configurations. Try larger specimen material such as fourteen-inch hanging baskets or twelve-inch clay bowls. Ask your grower for "straight up" plants, which means plants haven't been pinched off to

Who could resist this different poinsettia arrangement? The homey basket and pink bracts on the plant will stand out from your competitors' run-of-the-mill offerings.

encourage branching. Instead of one pinched plant with five average flowers, you get three plants with one giant flower each. Once virtually the only choice in the poinsettia market, straight ups have fallen by the wayside in recent years. Retailers who still offer them say they're getting as much as double the price of a standard six-inch pinched plant simply because straight ups offer a classier, more elegant look.

Sure, price is important, but remember—product differentiation is key to keeping consumers paying those higher prices.

In My Opinion, November/December 1997.

Will Consumers Pay More for Premium Poinsettias?

Laurie Scullin

While not all retail merchandising should be thought of in terms of a "war," the Christmas season, with its rush of customers, unpredictable weather, and fierce competition, does resemble a battlefield at times. In this contest, how can your side come out on top of poinsettia sales?

Pick Your Battles—Promotion versus Premium Quality

This is the first key strategic decision in the battle that your business is fighting. As the poinsettia crop has become a flash point in consumer pricing, your team must decide whether to price for value or price for quality.

This past season, several big-box chains sold 6-inch poinsettias on a "3 for $10" promotion. At the same time, many retailers went the other direction by asking growers to supply higher quality premium plants—6½-inch and 8-inch products grown with more space between plants. Premium poinsettias generally are given a greenhouse cultural regimen that allows for full bract expansion, yielding a larger, broader leaf that will show more color. Premium poinsettias also develop a strongly branched plant, holding their lower leaves better because they have access to more light in the greenhouse.

This past December, the Paul Ecke Ranch, Encinitas, California, conducted a price point test at several supermarket chains. The goal was to test the sell-through of a premium price poinsettia. We supplied 6½-inch poinsettias (three plants per pot) as straight up, unpinched plants. Each pot had three very large bracts versus the more traditional five to seven smaller bracts on a pinched 6-inch plant.

We asked the retailer to price the premium poinsettia plant at four dollars more per pot than their standard six-inch pinched plant. Here in Southern California, we saw a price difference of $10.99 versus $6.99. The premium plants were displayed next to the regular priced six-inch plants.

Generally the sell-through was strong. Some stores sold out in just a few days, and several store floral managers have the potential to convert up to 50 percent of their sales this year to this premium item.

Win-Win

Why the attraction to a premium poinsettia?

1. When presented a choice, many consumers choose to upgrade to a product with more color and larger flowers. Remember that poinsettias are used for decoration—color sells!

2. The consumer gets a solid plant grown with a minimal amount of stress. Less stress equates to a longer shelf life.

3. The grower is given a chance to grow a higher value crop. Rather than cutting corners to hit a promo price, the grower has new challenges of how to increase the quality.

4. The retailer is able to turn more dollars per square foot of floor space while reducing shrink.

Now the premium poinsettia strategy may not be for every retailer, and our market test was small and not completely without bias. But the question remains: Are we underpricing and undersupplying the quality needed in the poinsettia market? If, in fact, 50 percent of the market is looking for a higher quality product, and if the missing price point is as high as four dollars extra per plant, then in the 60 million pot poinsettia marketplace we are underserving the consumers to the tune of $120 million!

Off the Shelf, November/December 1997.

The Value-Price Equation

Dr. Marvin N. Miller

For our annual trip this year to analyze the poinsettia market, we chose North Carolina, visiting retailers and the growers who supply them to get a sense of market dynamics and trends. We traveled right after Thanksgiving, during the week poinsettia sales really start to increase. Both the North Carolina retail and production industries challenged our thinking on poinsettias.

On one memorable evening, we visited five chain-store retailers: two home improvement/hardware stores and three discounters in a two-to-three-square-block area of Charlotte. To our surprise, the best-looking poinsettia display was at the retailer who had offered the worst displays during many previous trips to other areas of the country.

The plants represented an outstanding value for the consumer. But it wasn't the six-inch poinsettia many chain stores use as a loss leader (although

The high-quality plant package—eight-inch plant, basket, and tag—as seen at store level (left), and as it would look after the consumer took it home. *Photos by Marvin N. Miller.*

the same store did offer six-inch plants for $2.97). Instead, it was an eight-inch pot, with three plants pinched. The pot was covered with foil and sleeved, and the poinsettia was presented in a green wicker basket with gold-painted pinecones hand-tied all around the basket. The presentation was capped off with a tag that included care instructions and the history of the poinsettia. This exceptional presentation was offered for $12.97 in a new display rack that had been customized with signage for poinsettia sales.

Other retailers in the area also offered six-inch poinsettias for $2.97, while some priced six-inch plants at $4.99 and $5.99. Some of these plants looked fresh and offered value. Others had been in the stores for "two-and-a-half weeks," according to one employee who was trying to clean up the yellowing leaves on plants in the display. "They only missed one or two waterings," she responded, when asked if it wouldn't be better just to discard the over-the-hill plants. Another retailer offered plants that had been around so long that their yellow centers (cyathia) were missing. Not surprisingly, prices did not necessarily relate to freshness or quality.

Contrast this to the story from Cary, a suburb of Raleigh. A supermarket was selling 8-inch poinsettias for $9.99 with just a pot cover and sleeve. Again, the pot contained three plants pinched, and the floor display was beautiful. In the same strip mall, a retail florist was selling 6½-inch plants.

The florist described the $25 presentation as "the plant, with foil, bow, and ting-ting." We judged the $9.99 supermarket plant as far superior in size, freshness, and overall quality. Other consumers might have a different perspective, depending on how highly they value ting-ting.

What has been happening in the marketplace to the poinsettia has been described by many as a "commoditization of the product." Some retailers are using poinsettias as loss leaders. Sometimes poinsettias are promoted this way because consumers might not otherwise visit the particular retailer during this time of the year. (How many people do you know undertake home-improvement projects near Christmastime?)

Some question the effect of such discounting on the poinsettia's image with the consumer. Certainly, more poinsettias are sold as a result of the lower prices, and some claim that those buying from deep-discounting retailers wouldn't otherwise buy the plants. In such an environment, "poinsettias may still be given as gifts, but more of them are going to the mailmen and fewer are going to grandmothers," notes one frustrated observer. "They've just lost much of their prestige."

Yet, at least some retailers are recognizing that consumers want value, and that value includes both cost and quality. Low price alone won't capture the consumer's loyalty. It's a basic marketing premise; unfortunately, not all retailers have applied this to the poinsettia.

Still, some are learning. Several buyers were refused when they tried to buy six-inch poinsettias at a price the growers deemed too low. The same buyers were able to buy larger plants (for higher prices) from the same growers. Ironically, in at least one case, the chain's buyer returned to the greenhouse to examine his contracted crop of larger plants and asked the grower why he hadn't been willing to sell six-inch plants. Sometimes they get it; sometimes they don't.

The trend of adding value seems to be quietly moving across the country, as more and more retailers seem to be selling increasing numbers of larger pots. And they're paying higher prices for the plants: The average USDA wholesale price reported for poinsettias sold in five-inch or larger pots has been rising steadily over the last several years. Observers agree this is not because prices have been rising per se, but because the mix of plants is moving to greater quantities of larger pots or because growers are adding value in other ways by altering the poinsettia package.

As for the retail florist, the argument has often been made that the consumer who buys from the chain store isn't the same person who buys from the florist. That argument may apply to florists and discount or home improvement stores, but almost all households shop for groceries. The florist shop's customers (or the gift's recipients) are likely to notice the difference between the plants or the prices offered at the supermarket. Perhaps the florist in Cary, North Carolina, has a ting-ting loving clientele, and maybe the florist will consider it a successful Christmas season if she sells only a few ting-ting-laden poinsettias, while the grocer two doors down sells hundreds.

In any case, the marketplace seems to be changing very, very quickly. Some retailers certainly are more aware of the consumer's price versus value equation. While some retailers may not even allocate the labor to water plants on display, smart retailers will continue to look for ways to add value that the consumer will appreciate and for which the consumer is more than willing to pay.

March/April 1999.

Poinsettias: Order Early and Often

Chris Beytes

Chicago political lore suggests you "vote early, vote often." Poinsettias are much the same: Order early, and order often.

That's the advice of Dr. Marvin Miller, market research manager for Ball Horticultural Company, West Chicago, Illinois. Marvin's company distributes poinsettia cuttings to growers throughout the U.S. and Canada. Just what does his "order early" advice mean?

Order Early

"It's very easy to 'niche' your offerings if you order early," says Marvin. Poinsettia growers often make decisions about varieties and colors soon after finishing the previous season's sales, then bring in plants in April and May to start next season's crop. By July, they've already decided how many of each variety and color to grow, and in what sizes.

If you want to sell an unusual variety, perhaps in a custom container, you need to let your growers know early so they can order it and schedule the numbers you need. This is especially important with new varieties that may be in limited supply or for large containers that need extra growing time.

Order Often

Many of today's popular poinsettia varieties have been bred to bloom early, which is perfect because customers are asking for plants even before Thanksgiving. But plants in full bloom November 20 won't be their freshest for December 20 sales.

If you want to stock fresh poinsettias right up to Christmas, ask your grower to stagger his production so your plants are coming into bloom on a weekly basis. He can do this by lighting early blooming varieties to delay flowering or by choosing later blooming varieties. Something else to remember: Novelty colors such as marble, pink, and the Jingle Bells types are in short supply after about December 15.

Off the Shelf, March/April 1998.

Don't Get Trimmed on Your Christmas Tree Order

Chris Beytes

Consumers bought more than 33 million fresh cut Christmas trees last season—did you get your share of the business? Will your customers come back next year, or were your trees nothing but brown needles by December 25? To ensure customer return, here's some advice from Bruce Niedermeier, a member of the board of directors of the National Christmas Tree Association (NCTA), and a tree grower with 480 acres in Wisconsin.

Develop a Relationship with a Grower

Because each grower has his own grading system and technique for shaping his trees, you need to visit your supplier personally to see what you'll be getting. "A good retailer can't buy without seeing the trees," Bruce says. He adds that successful Christmas tree retailers buy from the same grower year after year—this way, the grower knows what the retailer likes, and the retailer won't get any surprises when he receives his shipment. Bruce says you can get a buyer's guide from your state Christmas tree association. (Christmas trees are grown in all fifty states!)

When you visit a potential supplier, find out how he stores his trees. Bruce says a good grower will cut, wrap, and store his trees in the same day. Trees should be stored in the shade—either under large trees or under shade cloth. One grower he knows stores them standing vertically in a building.

Order Early

Place your order in June or July. Letting your grower know what you'll need for Christmas as early as possible allows him to plan his shaping and harvesting program. It will also ensure that you get the variety mix you need.

Research Your Market

If you're getting into Christmas trees for the first time, do some demographic research on your local market. According to the NCTA, most people buy their trees just a few miles from home. If you're selling in an affluent area with large homes, you'll need to stock larger, higher grade trees. Areas with large apartment populations need compact trees.

What's a good mix of varieties and sizes? Bruce suggests stocking about 50 to 60 percent firs (an upper end tree), split between balsam and Fraser fir. Of these, about two-thirds should be No. 1 grade, and one-third should be No. 2 grade. The rest of your mix should be spruces (a middle- to high-end tree) and Scotch and white pines (lower end trees). Mix in a few lesser grade firs and balsams for later sales, along with a few white and blue spruces. In top-grade trees, 7/8 foot is the most popular size, Bruce says, followed by 6/7 foot, then 8/9 foot and 9/10 foot.

Arrange Shipping

If you're ordering six hundred to eight hundred or more trees, shipping shouldn't be a problem, as a flatbed truck holds eight hundred to nine hundred trees, and a refrigerated truck holds about six hundred. For smaller orders, you may pay more, or you may have to arrange with another local seller to pool your shipments. Most important: Have a cool, shady spot prepared when the shipment arrives. No matter how good the trees look when delivered, storing them on hot asphalt or in the sun will dry them out and leave your customers shopping elsewhere next year.

Off the Shelf, March/April 1998.

Christmas Tree Care: Freshness Guarantee

Fraser firs have long held their place as America's favorite Christmas tree. Growing only in the southern Appalachian Mountains above 3,000 feet, these glossy, dark green trees exude a strong aroma and have soft needles that will stay on trees if properly cared for. And their resistance to shipping stress and temperature fluctuations makes them popular for retailers and consumers alike. Keeping Fraser firs and other trees fresh and customer-ready is easy with a few quick tips.

Contrary to popular belief, trees that travel long distances aren't any more prone to quality loss than locally grown trees, says Pat Wilkie, executive director of the North Carolina Christmas Tree Association. The way trees are handled on retail lots has a great effect on their freshness and quality. With retailers setting up tree lots earlier during the holiday season, proper care is even more important so trees will meet your customers' expectations for display life.

Store trees in shaded areas protected from temperature extremes and wind. Shade cloth, burlap, or boughs are more effective for covering trees than plastic, which lets light pass through to damage trees. Store and display trees standing upright rather than laying them flat on the ground.

Also, after trees are unbaled and displayed, spray them with water only during night or early morning to reduce the rate of drying, particularly in hot climates, Pat advises. Needles on fresh trees break crisply when bent sharply. Needles on trees that have lost a lot of moisture are more pliable and tend to bend without breaking.

Species that last the longest and remain the freshest include the North Carolina Fraser fir, Balsam fir, Scotch pine, and Douglas fir.

Off the Shelf, July/August 1997.

Elevate Your Christmas Tree Sales

Joli A. Shaw

Tired of propping up Christmas trees in cinder blocks or staking them to keep them straight? Here's an inexpensive, effective, and surprisingly simple way to display Christmas trees to their best advantage: Suspend them from your ceiling or greenhouse trusses. We saw this idea at Wannemaker's, Downers Grove, Illinois. Take a piece of twine (length depends on roof height), flip it over the truss, wrap it several times around the tree about one foot from the tip, pull the twine until the tree is suspended one or two inches off of the ground, and tie it in a loose knot that can be easily released in one motion.

This system offers several advantages for both customers and employees: It saves time in the selling process, as employees don't have to stand up or spin trees to show them off to customers. Customers can walk completely around each tree, which means they can see it from all sides. And suspending them allows both customers and employees to tell if a tree is truly straight.

Wannemaker's labels their trees in two ways: Each tree gets a tag near its middle—at customer eye level—that includes the price and species name. To ensure that customers can still find the price should the tag fall off, the trunk of each tree is spray painted with one of seven colors. Each color indicates a grade and price.

Off the Shelf, September/October 1998.

Christmas Tree Sales Strategies

Joli A. Shaw

What can you do at the store to help your customers' Christmas trees look good longer? A few simple strategies aimed at extra service and quality maintenance can add value to your tree corral. Here are some ideas from Emerald Christmas Tree Company, Bellevue, Washington.

- Trees without water remain fresh only one-third or half as long as trees with a fresh cut in a water stand. Unless freezing conditions exist, display trees in water after making a fresh butt cut.
- Make a fresh cut on all trees before they leave the lot. This gives the customer five to six hours to get the tree into water without having to make another cut.

- Recommend that trees tied to car tops be covered with plastic, tarps, or blankets to prevent wind damage or the tree's freezing to the car top. Offer garbage bags or rolls of plastic to sell or give to customers for this purpose.
- Encourage your customers to take the tree home in the trunk to lessen exposure to extreme temperatures.

Off the Shelf, November/December 1997.

Chapter 12
Once and Future Trends

Tracking Trends in the Popular Press
Chris Beytes

Nearly every one who sells plants also sells garden magazines. But how many of you actually thumb through them every month and apply what you've read to your own businesses? It's simple to do, and with a little imagination you can turn their hard work into free publicity for your own garden centers. Here are some tips to capitalize on the trends you see in popular magazines.

What's Read All Over?

Gardening magazines have tremendous influence on their readers. *Martha Stewart Living* Garden Editor Margaret Roach says, "When we list a source [for a plant] in the magazine, they sell out! And it's not just the experts buying; it's a lot wider group of people who are calling up that day when they read the article. Anything that we do, it sells out. It's amazing!"

Are any magazines better than others at reporting trends that fit your business and your customer base? Dozens of national titles are on newsstands; some are focused exclusively on gardening, such as *Fine Gardening, Organic Gardening,* and *Horticulture.* Some have gardening sections every month, along with style, home, cooking, and other topics, such as *Better Homes and Gardens* and *Martha Stewart Living.* Add to these regional and state magazines like *Southern Living, Midwest Living,* and *Sunset,* the special seasonal garden issues put out by *Woman's Day,* and other general interest magazines and the thousands of newspaper garden sections published every weekend in every city, and you have an abundance of free ideas waiting to be "borrowed."

Pinpoint Your Audience

Each of these magazines caters to a slightly different audience. A look at the ads gives each audience away. *Organic Gardening,* one of the most hard-core gardening publications, features ads for juicers, soil test kits, rototillers, composters and canning equipment. Compare these with such *Garden*

Design advertisers as Tiffany & Co., British Airways, Stolichnaya vodka, and Dooney & Bourke leather goods, to name a few.

The subject matter covered by each also reflects the readership's differences. *Organic Gardening*'s May/June issue has articles on controlling slugs and snails, choosing sunflower varieties, growing your own cherries, and planting perennial borders. *Garden Design*'s May offerings include a profile of a California landscape architect who incorporates her clients' secret dreams into their gardens, stylish containers, the comfort of fences, succulents, and espalier (training trees to grow flat against a support)—but nothing on slugs.

These are two distinct readerships with two distinct gardening goals. But despite the differences between the two magazines and their audiences, they both cover topics every gardener wants to know about— perennials, pots, pest control, fruit trees—they just present the information in different ways to fit their readerships.

Which audience shops at your retail establishment: the back-to-the-land *Organic Gardening* crowd, the elite *Garden Design* readers, or something in between? The answer will help you focus on what trends to highlight and how to highlight them.

However, don't inadvertently discriminate against your customers, thinking that they're either too upscale to read *Organic Gardening* or too lowbrow to subscribe to *Garden Design*. You want to pull ideas from both and track customer response. Margaret Roach says *Martha Stewart Living*'s gardening readership runs the gamut "from complete, absolute, utter beginner to very sophisticated and advanced."

Two's a Trend

Read through several different magazines, and you'll often see the same topics covered. *Garden Design* wrote about high-end containers in the May issue; *Fine Gardening*'s June issue also offers an interesting item on unique pots for container gardening. (Margaret Roach calls the container gardening trend "huge.") The May issue of *Garden Design* gives instructions on making bent-twig trellises; the June *Fine Gardening* tells you how to make small twig trellises for pots. Both *Southern Living* (June) and *Better Homes and Gardens* (May) wrote about daylilies, with *Southern Living* calling them "the ultimate perennial." One interesting trend is tropical gardens in temperate climates: *Fine Gardening*, *Garden Design* and *Southern Living* have done articles on the topic this spring.

Any time you spot common themes like these, it's a safe bet to put them to work in your business, making sure your signage points out: As Seen in *Fine Gardening* and *Garden Design*. Have copies of the magazines on hand, and even imitate some of the ideas shown in their photographs. Your customers will appreciate that you're keeping up with current trends and that you're helping them keep up, too.

Of course, as Margaret Roach points out, any time a popular magazine covers specific plants or topics, readers flock to local garden centers looking for them. Capitalize on this. If your business is in the South, stock and prominently feature anything that *Southern Living* writes about. If your local newspaper has a widely read garden writer, keep up with what he or she is writing about and set up a display highlighting the week's topic. You might even work with the writer to set the topic. If you operate stores in various cities, establish company-wide guidelines for the displays, but let store managers work with local publications to choose the week's focus for their particular store.

Weaving Trends Together

Often, the trends that magazines cover get their start elsewhere. It's no longer news that the textile and homewear industries have been capitalizing on the gardening theme. Sunflower-printed fabric and wallpaper helped boost sales in sunflower seed and plants. Sunflowers are still hot (experts say sunflowers aren't a trend, they're an integral part of Americana), but a new home decorating trend, according to Julie Wilkinson, Highland Supply's director of education and creative marketing, is romantic, cabbage-style roses and other flowers. In a seminar she presented at GrowerExpo '97, a floriculture industry conference held in Chicago, Julie mentioned that more and more fabrics were showing this theme. Less than four months later, the April *Fine Gardening* featured herbs planted with old roses; the April *Garden Design* featured floral-upholstered chairs, and the June cover of *Martha Stewart Living* showed Martha surrounded by roses in full bloom in her East Hampton, New York, garden.

Make regular trips to fabric and interior design stores, looking for upcoming trends that might relate to gardening. These industries work several years ahead and won't waste moneymaking designs they don't think will sell. Julie also recommends buying fabric or printed paper to use as backdrops for displays. It's a relatively inexpensive way to create an upscale look.

Whether you run one store or a thousand, capitalizing on topics covered by gardening publications is an easy way to gain an edge over your competition and give your business an upscale, trendy image. It's one thing to build a display of fancy pottery; it's another to include a laminated copy of *Garden Design's* article on the topic along with some of the same pots or ideas highlighted in the article.

Consumer Buzz, July/August 1997.

Capitalize on Past and Current Trends

J Saxtan

From Sélection Meilland Nederland B.V., Ouderkerk a/d, Amstel, the Netherlands, a major rose breeder, comes a look at current social trends that may influence consumer lifestyles and floral preferences. Five trends they have identified are:

1. Simplify—This is a reaction to, or an escape from, stressful situations. It's an interior with order, rest, and rhythm. The use of cool colors and native colors is central. Examples include vases set in one row, identical pots lined up, and anthuriums in bottles.
2. Revalue—This includes the revaluing of the past and accessories that reflect the "good old days," like old containers. The story, history, and background of the product are important. Examples include special arrangements in old containers, like those with nostalgic advertisements on them; the use of classic materials and garments in a different way or in fresh colors; the use of warm colors such as browns; and the feeling of luxury.

3. Revalue modern—The same as above, but more extreme, this trend is about using very old materials, such as a vase wrapped with fur.
4. Experimental—Not the "either/or," but the "why not?" This trend tries to satisfy the sense perceptions as much as possible, combining new forms and colors. Examples include aggressive colors with warm tints, transparent plastic, and very artistic flower arrangements.
5. New dimension—Presentation in a nonlogical way. Examples include mixing autumn and spring flowers, vegetables mixed with roses, dead materials combined with live materials, colorless next to very colorful, or short roses in a big pot.

Meilland also called upon the firm of De Block & Dekker, a consulting and marketing research firm, to identify past and future trends. These have been characterized with animal names:

- 1980, duck period—Or yuppie time, where business and money was very important. In that period, the duck, with the show and dazzle of its feathers, fits perfectly. Key looks of the period are: coolness, geometry, white pots, black leather sofas, and only one ficus in the corner of the room.
- 1985, bear period—This animal represents warm and cozy. Central at the time were wicker baskets, hydrangeas with big bows, pots with potpourri, and pinks and multicolors. As the bear period grew tougher, colored pots were replaced by terra-cotta, and the sunflower began to appear on the scene.
- 1990, dino period—Dinos are dead animals. In this period, dead, dry, and big materials were dominating arrangements and decorating. Florists used dried grasses, zinc watering cans, and big stones. In dino time, all "eco" concerns were very important. This was followed by the move from natural to unnatural and artificial.
- 1995, insect period—Translucent plastic, often in colors, was a theme. Thin and round forms, forms of animals, contrasting colors, and painted wicker baskets prevailed.

What's next? Wolf period? This animal lives a retiring and quiet life, and mankind is looking for more rest and safety. Freshness and a guarantee of freshness will play a big role.

Consumer Buzz, January/February 1998.

Sell More Flowers by Tracking Color Trends

Color sells fashion, whether it's apparel or home furnishings and accessories. Color also sells flowers. It makes sense to tie the two together, and a Danish grower has done just that to boost his mum sales to three million pots per year, according to mum breeding specialist Yoder Brothers Inc., Barberton, Ohio.

Yoder reports that grower Niels Pedersen consulted with a Danish fashion expert to explore ways to increase mum sales. Linda Noack, founder of Team Grow-how, a Danish company that specializes in fashion trends and forecasting for the flower industry, suggested that he change his product mix frequently, adding and dropping colors based on fashion trends and the seasons. Niels talked Denmark's two largest supermarket chains into letting him change their product mix regularly.

Upholstery and draperies on display at furniture stores can clue you in on what the hot colors and patterns will be.

Starting with lilac, rose, lemon-and-green, gold, honey, yellow, cream, and white mums, Niels changed his product mix seven times during 1997. This year he plans to change his mix thirteen times.

A Yoder spokesperson says that some of the purple tones that the Color Marketing Group has forecast as hot for 1999 (Mystical Purple, Freesia Purple, Pure Purple, and Regal Purple) will tie in perfectly with some of the pot mums they've bred.

For ideas you can put to work this weekend, learn which colors are hot in your area: just look in department store and home furnishings store windows to see what they're selling. Pay special attention to upholstery: Manufacturers won't invest in colors and designs that they don't anticipate will sell well.

Consumer Buzz, July/August 1998.

Can You Trust Color Trends?

Groups such as Cooper Marketing Group and Pantone Color Institute specialize in surveying consumer attitudes toward colors. Their survey results come out one to two years or more before when they think a trend might hit mainstream retailers, which could lead you to question their validity. But looking back proves that some projected color trends have come to fruition.

Take sunflower yellow, for instance. According to *American Demographics* magazine, Cooper's surveys were showing that consumers were beginning to favor bright yellow two years before sunflowers became such a popular household décor item.

In 1995, Cooper forecasted that terra-cotta and denim would be the next big colors. Sure enough, terra-cotta pottery is more popular than ever with today's gardeners, and many popular designer mixes of impatiens, petunias, and pansies all feature various shades of blue. In fact, according to one flower breeding company, one of the best-selling designer mixes in trend-conscious California is a blend of blue shades called Niagara Mix. And a new blue pansy from another breeder is named Denim.

Speaking of blue, it's the favorite color of 40 percent of men and 28 percent of women. But one of the fastest-growing color classes in gardening is pink and purple. Seventeen percent of woman say purple is their favorite color, compared to just 4 percent of men, which is important to remember considering that women make up the majority of garden consumers. At this year's new variety trials in California, breeding companies debuted a wide range of new varieties in various shades of pink, rose, fuchsia, lavender, and purple to satisfy the burgeoning consumer demand for these colors.

This brings up one last point: When placing flower orders, keep women's tastes in mind. Most men prefer red, while most women prefer pink. If a man places your geranium order, he may order too many reds compared to pinks because of his preferences. If they don't sell, you may incorrectly assume that customers don't want geraniums.

Consumer Buzz, July/August 1997.

Gardens Get Bold: Seven Trends for the Decade

As gardening continues to pick up momentum as America's favorite outdoor pastime, it's more important than ever to know what the garden trends are. In the spring 1999 issue of *Garden, Deck & Landscape,* horticulturist Marianne Binetti listed some of her picks for the next decade's gardening trends:

1. Colors—Colors are brightening up from soft pastels to bright, strong statements. Hot pinks, vivid yellows, bright oranges, and fiery reds bring energy to the landscape. Watch for foliage with colorful and variegated leaves, too.

2. Tropical plants— The tropical trend brings a vacation paradise to the home. Marianne suggests frost-tolerant bananas, cold-tolerant wind-mill palms, and cannas as popular possibilities. Winter-hardy, tropical-looking plants will sell.

Three trends in one garden (left): bright colors, vines, and garden structures. Lush plants such as cannas and caladiums (right) bring the trop-ics to temperate climates. *Photos by Netherlands Flower Bulb Information Center.*

3. Stonescapes— Rocks, boulders, and stones are becoming popular landscape items, sometimes as substitutes for plants. They're as low-maintenance as you can get and lead the eye

toward focal points. They can also liven up awkward corners and plant-free areas.

4. Vines—Vertical gardens are on the rise with trellises, teepees, wire supports, poles, and other structures. Climbing roses, jasmine, sweet-potato vines, and bougainvillea are her recommendations for small spaces, container gardens and walls.

5. Garden art—Gardeners are looking for benches, birdbaths, sundials, and birdhouses that are well designed and affordable.

6. Gardening as a lifestyle—To put it simply, this is a trend that means gardening will play a major part in how people define themselves: what they wear, where they travel, what they read, and with whom they spend time.

7. Gardening on the Web—The Internet will continue to bring people together, from plant collectors looking for a specific cultivar to the novice looking for expert answers to detailed questions. The Web is already allowing direct sales from the grower to the end consumer.

GrowerTalks, *In Brief, March 1999.*

Sunflowers Are a Tradition, Not a Trend

Worried that the sunflower fad is fading? Don't be. Trend experts classify sunflowers as a traditional part of the American landscape—they're an American icon. One clue is the amount of attention breeders pay to them. Several major seed companies have brought out new pot and cut varieties in the last few years.

Recently, at least two major consumer magazines have printed articles on sunflowers. *Organic Gardening* featured sunflowers on the cover of its May/June issue with an article "Grow the Sunniest Flowers of All!" The article credits Japan's Sakata Seed with developing the first pollenless sunflowers, which are "much better suited to cutting and using in arrangements." It also lists thirty-three different shapes, sizes, and colors of sunflowers suitable for home gardeners. The May issue of *Southern Living* features a "sunflower playhouse" at Georgia's Callaway Gardens with walls and roof made entirely from live, growing sunflowers. Check out both features to gather some ideas for great summer and fall sunflower promotions at your business.

Consumer Buzz, July/August 1997.

Potted Plant Trend Watch

Chris Beytes and Joli A. Shaw

With nearly $686 million worth of flowering potted plants sold at wholesale in 1996, interest in pot plants shows no sign of waning. From the old favorite chrysanthemum to newer choices such as aquilegia and cyclamen, pot plants are a must for many consumers' homes. Here we take a look at the latest trends and developments in today's pot plant market.

Bringing the Tropics Indoors

A big trend lately, according to Steve Bender, long-time garden writer for *Southern Living,* has been toward the bright, flamboyant colors of tropical plants. Hibiscus, *Mandevilla, Dipladenia,* stephanotis, and *Allamanda* are just a few of the tropical plants widely available in a wide range of sizes, from small pots for windowsills to large patio planters.

The state flower of Hawaii, hibiscus may be the most popular of the tropical flowering plants, especially in 6-inch or 6½-inch pots. They're available in a wide range of hot tropical colors, from yellows to pinks and peaches to rich reds.

The tropical flowering plants, if given a bright, sunny window, will continue to set new buds for months. Your customers' biggest challenges will be giving them enough light and humidity indoors during the winter months; once outside temperatures are above 50°F, they'll do well on a porch or patio.

Bulbs for Pots

Bulbs have long been a garden staple, but gardeners have also enjoyed bringing them into the home as flowering pot plants. With their increasing popularity, the bulb selection has become more diverse as breeders work to meet consumer demands. The wide range of bulb sizes available makes them good for containers in a variety of sizes, from three-inch mini pots to larger eight-inch and ten-inch pots. And because of the large number of bulb species, they can be used year-round (Asiatic and Oriental hybrid lilies) or as seasonal plants (spring-flowering tulips).

Perennial Favorites

Perennial plants such as aquilegia (also known as columbine) are the perfect gifts that keep on giving—enjoy them in the house, then plant them in the yard for years of enjoyment. Pictured is the variety Songbird.

Another trend in pot plants is perennials. Research by several leading universities now allows growers to force a number of perennial varieties into bloom at any time of year, rather than having to wait for their natural bloom time. A good example is campanula, a compact plant with attractive white or blue flowers. Other perennials that are sometimes sold as pot plants include aster, coreopsis Early Sunrise, Shasta daisy Snowlady, *Platycodon*, aquilegia Songbird and Cameo, and the popular fall garden mums.

While beautiful, perennial flowers rarely last well indoors. They perform best in cool temperatures from 50 to 60°F. Customers with a cool porch or sunroom will do well with them. During the early spring, when it's still too cold for annuals, pot perennials are a perfect way to brighten a front step or patio.

Miniatures

The latest craze in pot plants: miniatures in pots smaller than four inches—three inches or even two inches! Growers are encouraging gift giving and collecting with these tiny plants. Breeders are answering the demand with varieties with small leaves and flowers. Perfect for offices, windowsills, and as room accents, many plants are available in miniatures. Crops such as cyclamen, kalanchoe, azalea, chrysanthemum, and rose all have miniature classes. Cyclamen even have a midi class that's in between standard-size varieties and minis. And minis' size makes them perfect for merchandising as impulse buys next to the cash register.

Cyclamen

An up-and-comer in the world of pot plants, cyclamen has yet to reach its popularity peak. Species are available in three sizes—standard, midi and mini—and have been bred with interesting traits such as fringed or ruffled flowers and marbled foliage. Cyclamen are perfect for both fall and spring sales—they bloom from November to Mother's Day. Some breeders are even bringing scent into their varieties. Almost all of the varieties in Goldsmith Seeds' midi-size Laser series are scented.

With its marbled foliage and ruffled or fringed flowers, cyclamen will be gaining in popularity with your customers.

Hydrangea

Hydrangea plants have traditionally been seen with blue, pink, and sometimes white flowers. This has remained the standard for this winter/spring pot plant in the U.S. for many years, though European breeders have developed alternatives to the standards. Now it appears American breeders are also looking for unique hydrangea plants to pump up the market. New from Bay City Flower Company, Half Moon Bay, California, is Ravel, a bicolor pink and white hydrangea. Complete with an eye-catching metallic bronze-edged care tag, Ravel is a refreshing introduction to the pot plant market.

America's Sweetheart

The rose is nearly every gardener's favorite flower, and miniature pot roses are an easy way to bring the beauty and scent of a rose indoors. While the rose isn't the easiest blooming plant to produce or to maintain, consumer demand for pot roses has risen dramatically in recent years, leading breeders to develop a wide range of varieties with improved shelf life. Given good care, miniature roses can last for six or seven weeks indoors. They're available from growers pretty much year-round. Unlike pot perennials, miniature roses usually won't grow outdoors in the landscape—garden roses are grown on rootstock specifically chosen for garden performance.

Chrysanthemum

Chrysanthemum breeders' new introductions are paralleling color experts' trend predictions for 1998: whiter, brighter colors in softer, warmer shades of earthy reds, oranges, and golden browns. The Color Marketing Group predicts colors including Salmon Mousse, a softer, lighter orange; Ragin' Cajun, an earthy red influenced by orange and brown; Apache, a mix of red and brown; and Antigua Bear, a true golden brown. Recent color combinations from breeders follow these predictions, such as Pelee and Dark Bronze Charm from Yoder Brothers and Bronze Disco Time and Toffee Time from Van Zanten.

January/February 1998.

Pot Plants with Pizzazz: Mini Ficus

Laurie Beytes

Next time you pick up the phone to order some more ficus bushes, consider trying something that's a little out of the ordinary: miniature ficus. They're the perfect size to put anywhere a regular ficus bush would be too big to fit: table tops, windowsills, and shelves. And, they're too cute for your customers to pass up as an impulse item.

Standing a mere six to eight inches tall in four- or five-inch pots, they look like a dwarf version of the "real thing." Also, their tiny leaves are perfectly matched in size to their tiny stature. In fact, they give very much the same effect as a bonsai tree, but without all the work. They would lend themselves very well to being used for that purpose as well.

Mini ficus varieties grown at the Hermann Engelmann Greenhouses Inc., Apopka, Florida, are hybridized in Denmark. From there, plants are shipped to Engelmann's, potted up, and given approximately six months to acclimatize and grow out. After that, they're ready to be used as stock plants for propagation. Miniature ficus are slow growers, taking three times as long to grow as the large, more standard *Ficus benjamina*. A five-inch pot will finish in eight to nine months.

Engelmann's has been growing miniature ficus for the past three years and currently has eight varieties in production, with four more on the way. These are true varieties of *Ficus benjamina* that will always be miniature, regardless of their culture. And having been greenhouse grown under shade, they're already acclimatized to growing in the lower light conditions of your customers' homes. Try some of these miniature varieties on for size:

Pandora is compact with slightly curled, glossy green leaves.

Nina is a new variegated variety with mint green leaves trimmed in cream.

Nikita, another new variegated variety, has mint green leaves and a wide cream edge.

Nicoline has oval, glossy, dark green leaves and is a truly unique ficus variety.

Ninet is a striking, highly variegated variety that takes well to being trimmed.

Nightingale has lime green leaves with a contrasting dark green center for a very unusual foliage coloration.

Nicole has dark green leaves surrounded by a band of bright white variegation. New growth appears as a contrasting lemon yellow.

Dwarf Natasha, one of the newest varieties, has tiny, dark green leaves.

Live Focus, November/December 1997.

A Cut Above

Teresa Aimone

You could call them specialty cut flowers; you could call them the minors among the majors. They're old standards that are making a comeback, familiar garden flowers that have become the latest rage, and others that have caught consumers' eyes simply because they're new and different. Whatever name you call them, the flowers we're talking about are enjoying a wave of popularity that shows no signs of stopping.

Snapdragon

Snapdragon is bouncing back as a top-selling cut flower for good reasons: a wide color range, long-lasting flowers, and good consumer recognition.

Store spikes upright to prevent curvature—snapdragons are very sensitive to gravity. This can sometimes happen in a matter of minutes, causing a permanent bend near stem tips that significantly reduces flower quality. Using preservatives will give snapdragons longer vase life, but be aware that sugar uptake causes the spikes to stretch and florets to separate, reducing quality. Average shelf life at room temperature is six to eight days. Refrigerate at 32 to 33°F, and wrap flowers in plastic film for longer—seven- to ten-day—shelf life.

Asclepias tuberosa

Asclepias tuberosa, also called butterfly weed, is a perennial. Flower stems are long (about twenty to twenty-four inches), and the flower inflorescence is an umbel with many fragrant blooms. Orange is the most common color, though flowers can also be rose-purple. The dried fruits can also be used in flower arrangements.

Unlike other members of the Asclepias genera, *A. tuberosa* exudes little milky sap from its stems. Average shelf life at room temperature is eight to ten days.

Stems of *Godetia,* or satin flower, can have as many as fifteen blooms.

Godetia

Godetia, or satin flower, is native to the West Coast. Keep plants and foliage on the dry side, but remember that if plants are allowed to wilt, they will have permanently crooked stems after they recover.

Godetia stems can have as many as fifteen flower buds. Vase life of *Godetia* stems can be twelve to sixteen days, if treated properly. All flower buds should open to normal size. Flower preservatives containing sucrose will damage *Godetia* leaves and reduce shelf life. Clear water works equally well or better.

Gipsy Carnation

With its smaller blooms, wide color range, and distinctive fragrance, Gipsy carnation has proven to be another excellent bouquet filler flower.

Gipsy carnations have no waxy leaf layer, so be careful not to let water remain on the leaves, as this could cause leaf burn, particularly during the middle of the day. Water only late in the day or early morning.

Use a floral preservative and refrigerate flowers at 40°F.

Hypericum Flair

Hypericum is a rising star in the European cut flower industry. Within six years, the number of stems sold has risen by 1,200 percent, creating interest in countries such as Japan and the U.S. *Hypericum* isn't grown for its flowers but for its dark green foliage and bright red berries. Varieties in the Flair series have larger and brighter berries. Shelf life can be two to three weeks.

Limonium Hybrid

Several types of *Limonium* are available as cut flowers; most retailers and consumers are familiar with *Limonium sinuatum*. But these days, there is a new type of *Limonium* gaining interest. One in particular is from tissue culture, and its variety is the Misty series. These bouquet filler flowers have very long stems—up to forty-seven inches. Misty will bloom throughout the year if provided with the right temperature and light conditions. *Limonium* Misty can also be used as a dried flower. Refrigerate at 40°F, and store in a lighted area.

Orchidola

These miniature versions of gladiola have been nicknamed orchidola by the Israeli nursery industry. The petal shape and the variation in color patterns, similar to the orchid-flowered gladiolas of the 1960s, inspired the name.

Why are they so popular? Their short stems and smaller flowers make them lighter in weight and less expensive to ship. They are available in a wide, unusual color range.

Orchidolas bloom intermittently, like gladiolas. Note: Like snapdragons, place them in a preservative to open flowers quickly. Avoid warm temperatures, and refrigerate at 35 to 40°F. Shelf life should be seven to ten days.

Trachelium caeruleum

With its long graceful stems and open, airy flower heads, *Trachelium* make wonderful cut flowers. Trachelium is native to the Mediterranean. Flowers come in striking lavender and dark blue, as well as creamy white and pastel pink. While warmer temperatures will speed up flowering, they will

Trachelium most commonly displays dark blue or purple flowers. It is native to the Mediterranean.

also cause poor flower quality and thin stems. Plants can last ten to fourteen days. Place in water immediately after cutting.

September/October 1997.

Index